TIME
MANAGEMENT

TIME MANAGEMENT

An Introduction to the Franklin System

RICHARD I. WINWOOD

Franklin International Institute, Inc.
Salt Lake City, Utah

Franklin International Institute, Inc.
P.O. Box 25127
Salt Lake City, Utah 84125-0127

Printed in the United States of America

Printing number

8   9   10

ISBN 0-939817-07-1

Contents

To Richard, Julie, Sarah, and Steve

Acknowledgments

Having just reread this manuscript for the umpteenth time, I am impressed, and a little overwhelmed, by the enormous contributions by others to this book. Writing is a joy for me, most of the time. I am passionate about the subject of personal achievement, and I have a sincere desire to share —not so much what I know, but what I've learned. That learning has involved many, many people.

My first thoughts are of my wife, Judy, and our children. Anyone who gains anything from this book ultimately owes something to them. Aside from the laboratory for testing principles my family provides, they are the ones who ask, "Is Dad through with his book yet?" I deeply appreciate their patience with me.

The field of personal development is filled with great people. I've quoted from the work of more than a few in this book, but I want to give special recognition here to Paul J. Meyer, James W. Newman, Charles R. Hobbs, Alan Lakein, Alec R. MacKenzie, R. Dean Herrington, Edwin Bliss, Andrew Grove, and Michael LeBoeuf. I've been their student. They are the great ones.

At Franklin International Institute, Inc., there are a host of people who have helped me shape thoughts and concepts. I appreciate the insight and knowledge of Robert F. Bennett, Lynn G. Robbins, Dennis R. Webb, Greg Fullerton, Kevin Hall, and Arlen Crouch. It is a rare privilege to associate with such fine people. My assistant, Carol Force, has been an indispensable and constant support. Thanks also to Lynn Haslam for her help with the manuscript.

Hyrum W. Smith and I have proven so many concepts in consulting and in teaching these principles in this book over the years—to what has become a huge client base at Franklin. We have shared so many business "foxholes" that we are brothers, indeed. This book would not have been necessary or possible without his tremendous gifts.

My mother, Edna Enz Winwood Clark, used to read to me when I was a child. Fact, fiction, poetry, whatever. It was in those stories and poems that I first learned to dream, to see things in my mind that were beyond my circumstances. Thanks, Mom.

Finally, to the "crafty old sophister," Benjamin Franklin. I dream of meeting this old sage in a world removed from this one someday—just to say thanks, personally.

Foreword

It was Benjamin Franklin who said, ''Time is money.'' Consequently, I'm not sure you have time to spend browsing through this foreword. In fact, I'm not sure this book needs a foreword at all. The ''good stuff'' is inside.

You still here?

Then let me tell you about this book and something about the man who wrote it. The contents of this book have been developed over a period of years—ever since the Franklin International Institute, Inc., has been in existence. Most of the material is the result of experiences in the ''field'' teaching time effectiveness principles to business corporations, governmental agencies, educational institutions, and a host of other organizations all around the world—to date, almost a million people.

The seminar we started with was much different from the one that over a hundred seminar leaders in the Franklin Time Management seminar teach today. We believe it's much better today. A recent university study showed that the average person who had attended a Franklin Time Management seminar had increased their daily effectiveness by over 29 percent. The return on investment that we provide for our clients is enormous.

In this book, Dick Winwood has written down the principles we teach, in a way that only he can. He has a way of catching the essence of an idea and

then expressing it so that it sticks in your mind—
always with the distinct impression that *you* can do
it, that you *can* accomplish your goals. It's a gift,
really. As you read the book I know you'll get a
feeling for the sense of excitement that Dick brings
to his subject. I think one of the reasons why Dick
is such an effective writer is because he cares so in-
tensely about getting his readers to not only learn
the principles he writes about but also to try them,
apply them, and gain the benefit they contain.

Another thing. I'm convinced that no one
knows more about the subject of time management
than Dick Winwood. It just rolls off his tongue
when he speaks about it, but I know the price he's
paid in research, study, and application. He's en-
cyclopedic about it. He knows it. He lives it. He
teaches it. And, once again, he's written about it.

I'm confident that you don't have many things
to do that are more important than reading this
book. I hope you get started right away. Hurry,
''Time is money.''

HYRUM W. SMITH
Chairman of the Board
Franklin International Institute, Inc.

1

A World of Time

"In the beginning. . . ." The opening line of the most
famous book in all history, heard so many times, in so
many languages, by so many people has become passé.
The full meaning and significance of the phrase is seldom
discerned. It is obvious that with the first words of
Genesis we have been taken from the realms of the in-
finite and placed in a world of the finite. A world of
beginnings and endings. A world of Time.

Lynn Grant Robbins

Look in your purse or pocket. Go to your desk
or the front of your refrigerator. Find your calendar
and flip through it. Twelve pages. Twelve months.

A parcel of time. Seasons. Weeks. Birthdays. A cycle of time in its fullness. One complete revolution of the earth around the sun. That packet of lined and numbered pages was invented by our ancestors, as was Stonehenge, to subdivide the course of the sun.

Times and seasons were marked by the ancients for practical as well as mythical reasons. Time to plant. Time to celebrate. Time to gather together. Time to trade. It was "time," in the Pacific Northwest, when the thimbleberries turned red, for tribes to gather, to dance, to trade, to marvel. A tradition broken only by the encroachment of the white man—first into territory, then into tradition. The cycle of the thimbleberry continues, but the Indians no longer gather.

Many similarities exist today in the way we fashion our days and weeks. Our calendar might come from our friendly and ever-present insurance salesperson, but the arrangement of days, weeks, and months is still based, with minor variations, on the same solar cycle observed by the ancient Mayan.

Why the ancients wanted to understand and keep track of time, we can only guess. However, studies of the lives of all early peoples indicate basic similarities to modern cultures. They probably wanted, beyond the basic yearning for knowledge, to get more done. To produce more. To have more to trade. To anticipate better. To make better use of this thing we call time.

In today's world we search for ways to improve our lot. We want more happiness, goods, services. We want more time to enjoy the resources of this planet. To learn. To grow. To give.

It's a fact that some people seem to have an inside track on time effectiveness. While some seem to accomplish significant things and still have "free" time available, others of us seem constantly pressured by time and get done very little that's important. What is the difference? Is there a secret? There is definitely a difference. The difference is in how well we understand and use the precious resource of time. Time management is a skill to learn and apply.

TIME MANAGEMENT

Everyone is aware that time is a limited resource. Whatever we accomplish, we accomplish in the 168 hours we have available each week. Benjamin Franklin once observed that "to love life is to love time. Time is the stuff life is made of." Yet, with all our knowledge about its value, we waste a good deal of this crucial commodity.

What is time? Do you know? To most of us, defining time is an academic and seemingly worthless task. However, if we are to change the way we manage our time—or use it more wisely—we need to gain a clearer understanding of what time is. The key to understanding and using most basic resources is in understanding their basic elements. So it is with time.

TIME

"Time has no independent existence apart from the order of events by which we measure it" (Albert Einstein). Gottfried Leibniz, a German mathematician and philosopher of the early 1700s, after doing major research in the subject of time, observed that "time is merely the order of events, not an entity itself." In other words, time does not exist as a substance—you can't fill a bucket with it. Time exists only as an aggregate of events that have happened, are happening, or will happen in the future.

Webster's dictionary gives another clear definition of this idea. He says: "Time is a continuum in which events succeed one another from past through present to future." The continuity in definition from Leibniz to Einstein to Webster is in the word "events." Events are the basic element of time.

EVENTS

An event, according to Webster again, is simply a happening or occurrence of something. Events can be great or small, simple or complex—a war, a game, a play, a thought, a whatever happens. If you look at your watch and observe that it is 9:23 a.m., whatever is happening in that moment is an event.

Event Control

In his classic book *The Effective Executive*, famous management consultant and theorist Peter F. Drucker suggests that the task of the time manager is to *control* time where he can. Alan Lakein, in his book *How to Get Control of Your Time and Your Life*, states that *control* is the key concept in time management.

Having established that the basic element of time is an event and that control is the key to personal productivity or time management, let's take the obvious step of combining the two into a new definition for our management of time—*Event Control*.

The basic concept here is that all of us must realize the need to be proactive in achieving control in our lives as it relates to the events that make up our lives. The alternative is to simply react—to be acted upon, to let other influences decide for us what we will accomplish, to be controlled instead of in control. Personal event control suggests that we can decide for ourselves to what degree we can achieve success and in what areas of interest.

Controlling Events

Certainly there are events that are beyond our control; it would be foolish to assume omnipotence in this newly found event control idea. Some events happen whether we like them to happen or not—whether we would will them or not. Can we control the weather? The stock market? The down-time of the company computer? No. Neither can most of us control the culture in which we work, or other people's behavior. The only thing most of us get to control about these events is our personal responses to them.

We can choose to be upset by them. We can choose to be negatively preoccupied for hours over the rain falling on our personal parade. We can let the uncontrollable events in our lives worry us to the extent that eventually little holes are eaten in our stomachs. Or, we can choose to accept these kinds of events for what they are and make an appropriate adaptation. One of the vital principles of effective time management is learning to adapt when we face events which are beyond our control. Much of the stress we experience in our lives is a result of inappropriate responses, failure to adapt, to events.

Dr. Hans Selye, in his book *Stress without Distress* writes that "[the] great capacity for adaptation is what makes life possible on all levels. . . . Adaptability is probably the most distinctive characteristic of life."

It is, of course, of less importance to adapt when we face events over which we have a high measure of control. Here is a rich area for us to consider. The alternatives for growing, learning, and contributing are enormous. Our ability to choose, to decide for ourselves, is virtually unlimited. We have total control, for example, over our personal attitudes, to decide what's for dinner or what we are doing for vacation. More significantly, we can decide to a large measure what we will accomplish this year. What we will learn. How we will help. The opportunities for control in our personal lives are limited only by our thoughts.

CONDITIONING

Most of us can intellectually relate to some very basic facts of human potential. We know that we live in a world that has an abundance of opportunity available—literally on every hand. We also know that as members of the human family we have powers and capacities far beyond those which we use. Science is forever unlocking treasures of knowledge about the mental and physical capabilities of us earthlings. Recent studies indicate that even the most brilliant among us use something less than 15 percent of our reasoning powers. It's a sad fact that most brains are delivered to the cemetery plot hardly used at all. With all this innate potential, why are so many of us unsuccessful? Why do so many fail to catch a vision of personal possibilities? Why are we satisfied with so little when so much opportunity is available?

Part of the answer to these questions lies in our individual conditioning experiences. Many of us have literally been conditioned to accept less than we can have and to be less than we can be.

Several years ago I took my daughter Sarah to a traveling circus. As we approached the large tent that had been erected for the show, Sarah noticed an elephant behind the tent. "Can we go see the elephant?" she asked. I explained that we would be seeing elephants in the show and it wasn't necessary to go behind the tent to see them. That wasn't a good enough explanation, for some reason, so after much haggling, we walked together to the back of the circus tent to observe elephants at close range. When we got to where the elephants were, I was surprised to find eight elephants back there! Each elephant was tied up by a small rope which was attached to a ring on an iron manacle around each elephant's right rear leg. This small rope was, in turn, tied to a much larger rope that ran along the ground and was staked at either end. It occurred to me that any of these animals, huge and strong as they were, could easily have walked away from their harnesses to explore the shopping mall across the highway. In fact, everything I thought I knew about elephants told me that they were intelligent and curious enough to *want* to be free to roam around. But these didn't, and I wondered why. Later I made an effort to find out why these and lots of elephants just like them stay tethered when they have the power to move about.

I learned that, when very young, these elephants are chained by the right rear leg to immovable stakes. For several weeks they struggle to free themselves—they want to be free! Little by little —over a period of three or four weeks—the elephants are conditioned to believe that they can't move about when they are tied up by the right rear leg. From the moment that this conditioning influence takes hold—it doesn't matter what you tie them up with. They won't move. The elephants at the circus didn't roam about because they didn't *believe* they could. They didn't *think* they could. The tethers in their minds are stronger than any chain or rope.

We're not elephants. We're smarter than that. However, in many subtle ways, each of us has been conditioned to believe certain things about ourselves that limit us. Negative conditioning gets to all of us in some way. In short, there are events we don't control, things we don't accomplish, contributions we don't make, all because we don't *think* we can. In much the same way as the elephant, we too are tied to artificial stakes of the mind.

The concept of event control has great power as we begin to separate fact from fiction about our capabilities. As a result, some of the effects of conditioning melt away. With the artificial tethers removed, we can begin to see the future as an opportunity for self-fulfillment, an opportunity for grand experiences and service that *we* plan for ourselves. It's stunning insight, indeed.

THE BENEFITS OF EVENT CONTROL

Psychological theorist Nathaniel Branden, author of the book *The Psychology of Self-Esteem*, has said, "Productive work is the process through which man achieves that sense of control over his life which is the precondition of his being able to fully enjoy the other values possible to him." Kenneth Blanchard and Spencer Johnson in *The One Minute Manager* have stated a similar principle in another way, "People who feel good about themselves produce good results." The direct relationship between our sense of self-worth and our personal productivity is a relatively new concept in management. In time management, because its basis is personal productivity, the relationship is vital. A person may possess many practical skills and be able to apply them well and yet have a very low self-esteem. This person may feel a great discomfort at the thought of having to learn a new skill or having to change his environment in any meaningful way. Another person with a high self-esteem may be lacking in practical skills but, having no fear of learning or of confronting a new environment, can quickly and enjoyably learn and adapt to different situations. In the latter example, the person has confidence in his or her ability —based on a healthy self-esteem.

In other words, your personal self-esteem has a direct bearing on your ability to accomplish your wishes in life. Also, your self-esteem is enhanced when you are in control of events and it suffers when you are not in control.

Do you remember the first time you tried ice skating, skiing, or some other sport that required some basic level of physical coordination and experience to master? You probably felt awkward and out of control. You may even have been encouraged by your feelings to abandon your idea of learning this new skill. But, you stuck it out until you could make it around the rink or down the hill without falling. As you developed a basic skill level, your confidence grew and you began to enjoy the new feelings of control. This same idea can be applied to any new skill we desire to learn or any new experience we would like to have. Our first deliberate steps in this process are the most difficult and we often fall. However, as our ability to adapt to and then control ourselves within the new skill is strengthened, we enjoy what is now an exhilarating event. The nature of the event did not change, but our ability to control it, and thereby enjoy it, did.

At a seminar I taught some years ago to a large electronics firm, an engineer told me that at the end of the day she may add a task to her daily list *after* she had completed it. Then, acting as if the task had been on her list all along, she would check it off. "Why would you do that?" I asked her. "Because," she said with a wink, "I'm not going to get cheated out of the good feelings that come when I check a task off my list!"

I've often related that experience in seminars since and have been less than surprised to learn that thousands of others do the same thing on a daily basis—we usually don't talk about it much, but we all have similar feelings. We recognize that it feels good to be in control. We are healthier, happier, more effective, and more productive when we are in control. An interesting fact about the relationship between control and productivity is the way they tend to "feed" each other. When we feel good about ourselves we do good work, and when we do good work we feel good about ourselves.

The simple graphic here illustrates how the elements of Event Control, Productivity, and Self-Esteem fit together.

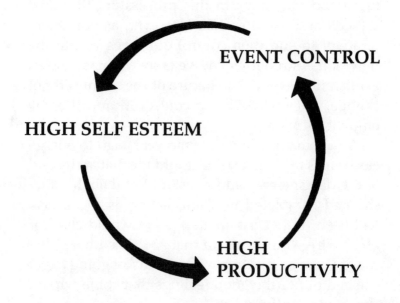

EVENT CONTROL

HIGH SELF ESTEEM

HIGH PRODUCTIVITY

The model illustrated works whether the elements are productive or destructive. For example, when you put yourself in a condition of control, your productivity improves. As a result, your self-esteem is enhanced. Conversely, when you are out of control with the events in your life, both your productivity and your self-esteem suffer. What results, then, whatever the input, is a cycle spiraling you upward to higher levels of achievement or downward to an opposite outcome.

The idea, of course, is to stay in control to the extent of our ability, and if we find ourselves off the control path we should pause and put things in order for ourselves, remembering the necessity to adapt.

Gaining control of events that will strengthen us and help us to achieve our highest priorities is what this book is all about. It may be obvious by now, but the concept of time management presented here goes far beyond the list making and prioritizing that typifies books on this subject. As you move forward you'll see more evidence of this. Benjamin Franklin, a champion of personal productivity, once said, ''Doest thou love life? Then do not squander time, for that is the stuff life is made of.''

Life is made up of time. Those who can recognize their individual ability to control that time through the events that make it up will live happier, fuller, more productive lives. It's really your choice. Someone has said, ''If you fail to control the events in your life then events in your life will control you.''

It's about time.

2

Planning—
The Key to Control

The concept of control through plans and schedules is fundamental to sound management and to increased effectiveness.

Moore

How many more years do you expect to live? When you die, how long will you be dead? LeBoeuf asks these questions in his marvelous book *Working Smart*. His intention is to remind us of our mortality. (It worked on me!) We can waste our money and we're only out of money, but when we waste our time we've lost a portion of our lives. We gain control of our lives through planning. In fact, the life we have offers two wonderful gifts—time, and the ability to choose how we spend it. Planning is the process of choosing from our options.

In chapter one I quoted the Webster's dictionary definition of time. "A continuum in which events succeed one another from past through present to future." In this definition, three different types of events are mentioned—historical, current, and future. Planning is clearly associated with the future events.

PLANNING IS PREDETERMINING FUTURE EVENTS

Most people don't think they can predict the future. But, that's sort of what we do when we plan —we put control on future events. The realization of these future "planned-for" events comes about as we follow our plan.

Daily planning is such a simple idea and it's been around for a long time. Probably one of the earliest and most well-known stories of the effect of planning as a management discipline concerns Charles Schwab, then president of Bethlehem Steel. In a discussion with a management consultant one day, Mr. Schwab hurled this challenge. "Show me a way to get more things done with my time and I'll pay you any fee within reason."

Ivy Lee, the consultant, handed Mr. Schwab a piece of blank paper. "Write down the most important tasks you have to do tomorrow and number them in order of importance," said Lee. "When you arrive in the morning, begin at once on number one and stay on it till it's completed. Once you've completed the first task, recheck your priorities and begin number two. Stick with your task all day if necessary — as long as it's the most important one. If you don't finish all your tasks, don't worry. You probably couldn't have done so with any other method, and without some system you'd probably not even decide which one was most important. Now, make this a habit every working day. When it works for you, give the idea to your management. Try it as long as you like. Then send me your check for what you think it's worth.''

It is reported that some weeks later, after the idea had been tried and found worthy, Mr. Schwab sent Ivy Lee a check for $25,000 — an enormous sum for the thirties — along with a note saying that the idea was the most profitable one he had ever learned. Schwab also formulated a plan for all Bethlehem Steel management, using Lee's idea, that was carried out under his direction. This planning idea was given credit for turning Bethlehem Steel into the biggest independent steel producer in the world at the time. When asked by his friends how he could justify such a handsome sum for such a simple idea, Mr. Schwab asked, ''Aren't all ideas basically simple?'' Upon further reflection Schwab stated that the $25,000 was probably the most valuable investment that Bethlehem Steel had made that year.

Planning is a simple idea. It's an idea that is taken for granted by most people and practiced, in my experience, by very few. What daily planning most people do is in the shower or on the commute, mentally reviewing what the day may hold. Others, a much smaller group, make "to do" lists with some regularity. The list is usually jotted down on a yellow pad or the back of an envelope someplace. And, depending on the interruption level of the list maker, these lists, commonly made on Monday, are still good on Friday.

If planning is the key to control and if it's such a simple idea, why do so many people ignore it? I began asking that question of seminar participants some years ago. Why don't most people take the time to plan? Here are the answers, along with some of my comments:

1. *I already know what I have to do. Why take time to plan?* There are always routine tasks that need to be accomplished. Sometimes, depending on our job, these routine tasks can take up a significant portion of our day. However, our goals for achievement —both on and off the job—need attention. If you truly ask yourself what you want out of life, what you want to accomplish with your family or career, etc., many tasks will surface that are not a routine part of your day. For these types of future events, a daily plan is necessary—even vital.

2. *Planning doesn't work for me. I have too many interruptions.* Most of us have had the ex-

perience of walking into our offices in the morning and before we can get to our desk or even take off our coat, someone notices us and says, "There's Nancy now. Nancy, will you come over here, we need your help right away!" Some days are like that. Also, some of us have a much higher level of interruption to deal with on the job than others. It's a problem for planning, but still a poor excuse for not planning.

In an environment where we have multiple and frequent interruptions we need to plan carefully to make sure our plan is reasonable — that the number of tasks, or rather the time needed to accomplish them, is appropriate to the amount of time available. If you are apt to have limited time to focus on tasks, make your list short and break down tasks into small elements.

3. *I feel "tied down" when I have a long list of things I have to do.* That's natural. No one likes the thought of facing an overwhelming list of tasks. The solution, however, is not to avoid planning but to make your plans meaningful.

Then remember that the list is not in control — you are. Be flexible with your plan.

Occasionally we all need 'downtime'. It isn't absolutely necessary to have a list *every* day. However, those days will be the exception. The daily plan is a way to keep you on track to your goals and focused on your priorities—it's your daily control medium. View a daily plan as your ticket to success. It's a friend—not a foe. Remember, planning puts you in control and a by-product of control is freedom.

4. *I don't have time to plan.* If you feel this way you're not alone. Several years ago a study of senior executives found that 72 percent believed they lacked sufficient time to think or plan. It's a fallacy though. The fact is that we all have all the time there is. When we don't have time for an event or activity we are obviously giving our time to something else. Once the significant return for time spent in forethought and planning is understood, time ceases to be a major problem. Edwin Bliss, author of *Getting Things Done*, has said: "The more time we spend on planning a project, the less total time is required for it. Don't let today's busywork crowd planning time out of your schedule."

5. *I don't know how to plan properly.* Most people don't. The advantage to someone with this response is that they *know* they don't know. Many people assume, be-

cause they make an occasional list, that they know how to plan.

For all those who have questions about the steps in effective planning, here's a list of the most important considerations that should be a part of formulating our daily task lists:

1. *Find a place to plan that is relatively free of distractions.* Planning time is thinking time. Most of us can think more clearly if we can have a period of near or total solitude. For most of us, that will be our office before our day begins or perhaps late in the day just prior to departing for home. If the office isn't a good spot, you might consider a time before you leave home or later in the evening.

2. *Review your long-range objectives.* It's easy to get caught up on trivial things and lose sight of future event plans. Daily planning time is an opportunity for us to glance through our goals and ask ourselves, "What specific tasks can I do today that will bring me closer to my goal?" Make sure that every day your task list contains a step to help you accomplish your dreams.

3. *Make sure the number of tasks and the amount of time required by each is well within the time available in your day.* We have a tendency to

overplan our day. As a result we often feel defeated by our list before we begin or defeated at the end of the day because our planned-for tasks aren't anywhere near completed. I would suggest an easy rule of thumb. Do a quick review of the appointments you have on your calendar—see how much time you'll have for your list. Then factor in another 50 percent to take care of the unexpected interruptions you know will happen but can't plan for. Now, plan for the amount of time you have left.

4. *Set specific daily goals.* Be very specific in describing your tasks. Vague tasks foster vague responses. Specificity kindles specific action.

5. *Anticipate obstacles.* You needn't approach the day negatively, but you should do a "quick think" about the prospects for unscheduled happenings in your day. Try to foresee situations that could be a problem in keeping you from achievement. Then, plan around them—or at least have an appropriate response to them. It's like doing a radar sweep of the horizon to see if anything out there could do destruction to your day.

6. *Prioritize your tasks.* This final key is vital. Even with all the safeguards listed in this section there will be times when some un-

foreseen event will leave us short of check-marks at the end of the day. This needn't be cause for concern—it was obviously something that couldn't or shouldn't have been avoided.

But let's say you listed twelve things on your task list and because of the unanticipated cataclysmic event you only accomplished five. Well, that's good if the five represented your highest priorities for the day. It's not so hot if they represented your lowest. Prioritizing helps us to see at a glance which tasks give the highest payoff. Failing to prioritize leaves our task selection up to our emotions of the moment. Like "impulse buying" our emotional task selection may not be the wisest use of our time.

Take Time to Sharpen the Saw. . . .

Stephen R. Covey, in *How to Succeed with People*, talks about planning as "taking time to sharpen the saw." He states: "The more rushed we are, the more time we better spend planning our time and actions. Otherwise we become like the frantic driver who is too much in a hurry to go two miles out of his way to take the freeway and who then proceeds to burn himself up, rushing, then cussing every red light and every slowpoke on the old highway."

An interesting analogy, indeed.

3

Prioritizing— Laser Thinking

Since not all tasks are created equal, the organized executive must set priorities: that is, establish a hierarchy of importance, and match the commitment of time and resources to the relative importance of each task.

Stephanie Winston

In financial management there is an investment term commonly used called "opportunity cost." Opportunity cost is a simple way of helping us to understand that once we choose to make an investment in one alternative we automatically lose the opportunity to invest in any number of other alternatives.

So it is with time. When we decide to spend our time participating in one activity or event, we decide at the same time not to spend our time doing other tasks. Part of taking time to plan is, clearly, a process of prioritizing: deciding which task will give us the greatest return on investment.

PRIORITIZING IS IDENTIFYING THE VALUE AND ORDER OF EVENTS

When most people think of prioritizing they think of ordering activities—doing this thing first, this second, etc. Since prioritizing is, as stated above, a process of choosing based on return, effective prioritizing involves carefully considering the value of each task as well as the order it is to be given.

RETURN ON INVESTMENT (ROI)

Another common financial term is "return on investment" or ROI. When we have a financial investment to make we will always carefully consider alternatives, seeking the investment that provides the greatest return with the least amount of risk and the highest liquidity. To do otherwise would not be considered wise in money matters.

Benjamin Franklin once said that "time is money." While time certainly isn't money (and Ben *knew* that!), we get his point that time has great value and should be managed accordingly. In fact, the same type of analysis we give to investing our money we should give to investing our daily allotment of time. Imagine that each day you receive a "check in the mail" for twenty-four hours. When we consider the use of that twenty-four hours we should weigh how we can get the best return on investment from our use of it.

LASER THINKING

A laser is a narrow concentration of energy that can be directed for a productive purpose. "Laser thinking" is a way for us to focus our thinking and concentrate our energies upon our most important priorities until they are completed. When we concentrate our energies on our most important (high ROI) tasks we are using maximum power.

Several years ago in Portland, Oregon, my young daughter befriended a girl in her class at school. She was in our home quite often and we enjoyed having her around. It was obvious that Shelly came from a family that didn't have much in the way of material things. The clothes she wore told us and so did she, in an honest and forthright way common to young children. In time I met and got to know her father. He was a laborer who worked at a large company that dismantled ships for scrap metal.

One day I saw him at the store and he excitedly told me that he had decided to become a dentist. A dentist! How on earth was he going to become a dentist? That was my thought, but I nicely congratulated him and went about my business. A dentist, indeed. No way, I thought.

Later I heard that he had applied to dental school but was turned down because what college credit he did have wasn't enough and his GPA was too low. I figured that would be the end of it. Next, I learned that he had enrolled at the local college night school in order to bring his credits and GPA up to a necessary level. Would this guy never learn? Shortly thereafter I moved my family to Seattle for two years. Then we were off to Maryland for another two-year assignment. A year or so after that we were back in Portland again. From here you can probably forecast the rest of the story.

Walking through a shopping mall one day I happened upon Shelly's father. He looked good. Tall. Dressed nicely. I was reluctant to ask, but finally got up the nerve.

"You were thinking about dental school when we saw you last. Did you ever do anything about that?" I asked.

"Oh, yes," he replied. "I graduated last year from dental school. I now have a few months before I receive my specialty in orthodontics. It's been tough, but it was worth it."

As I walked away from that meeting I mulled over the wonderful effect of "laser thinking"—focusing energy on a future, planned-for event. Once we can decide on what is *really* important and pay the price for it in time and effort we can accomplish great things. Prioritizing our time works.

IDENTIFYING VALUE

Using the symbols A, B, and C as a way of designating priority is a notion that is as old as time management itself—and a key to laser thinking. Alan Lakein, in his classic book *How to Get Control of Your Time and Your Life,* popularized this A B C method.

It's simple. We all recognize that an A is more important than a B, a B is more important than a C, and so on. But, when we prioritize our daily tasks, our lifetime goals, or whatever, it is important that we have specific guidelines for the use of these prioritizing designators.

What is an A? A's represent your highest priorities. They *must* be done. A's are crucial, vital, critical. They provide the highest return on investment and therefore should never be procrastinated or ignored. A tasks are relatively few in number—finding them and identifying them is a key to effective time management.

Next is the B. B tasks are important. They *should* be done—but only after we have completed the A's. B's provide a high return and deserve our attention in their proper order. You should find that B's outnumber A's on your list 2 to 1.

C's come in last. C's *could* be done, but they are strictly "back burner" stuff. There are oodles of

C's. The C task has value, but it is limited and provides a significantly lower return than either A's or B's.

What about D's? Well, I would hope you never consciously plan to do a D. D's are a clear waste of time.

THE VITAL FEW AND THE TRIVIAL MANY

Notice in the explanations above that the volume of tasks increases as we move down the priority scale. There will always be more C's than A's. Joseph Juran, author on various management subjects, refers to this phenomenon as the vital few and the trivial many.

THE TYRANNY OF THE URGENT

It has been said that "if it weren't for the last minute, nothing would get done." There's some truth to this humorous statement. The reason we often find ourselves waiting until the last minute to finish or even start a task is because the task does not become *urgent* until the last minute. Other times, an urgent but unimportant task gets in the way of a vital, less urgent one. That is the tyranny of the urgent.

Charles E. Hummel, former president of Barrington College once observed:

The important task rarely must be done today, or even this week. The urgent task calls for instant action. The momentary appeal of these tasks seems irresistible and they devour our energy. But in the light of time's perspective their deceptive prominence fades. With a sense of loss we recall the important tasks pushed aside. We realize we've become slaves to the tyranny of the urgent.

We are so aware of the urgent. The urgent screams. The urgent rings. The urgent says "Do me now!" All this would be fine if these tasks were high, vital priorities. Unfortunately they seldom are.

URGENCY = PRIORITY

Many vital, must-do tasks have very little urgency associated with them. For example, when I conduct a seminar on time management, I commonly create a hypothetical situation where we suddenly have twenty-five hours in the day instead of twenty-four. An extra hour each day. I ask the participants to write down what they would do with it if they had an extra hour every day for the rest of their lives. Actual wording of the question includes this modifier: "What you would do must be something that is not getting done now to your satisfaction."

I have found a great commonality in the things people write down. Ninety-eight percent of the time they will mention three areas of interest:

1. *Physical well-being.* Exercise, sports participation, getting more sleep, etc.
2. *Intellectual well-being.* Reading, studying (homework), learning, skill development (music, etc.), artwork, etc.
3. *Relationship development.* More time with spouse, more time with children, more time with relatives, more time with friends, etc.

When I ask them to prioritize these potential time use activities, they almost unanimously say they are all vital, must-do tasks. They just don't have time to give them appropriate emphasis in their lives if we are limited to only twenty-four hours.

When you consider that the average adult American spends twenty-five hours or so in front of the television set each week, it makes the excuse that we don't have time to read, play, love, give, etc., a pretty frail one for most of us.

What vital tasks or areas of your life are being wasted because of a lack of urgency? Are you ready to start that exercise program you've been thinking about? Perhaps you've promised to spend more time with your family, but "just haven't had the time." You know about a series of cassette tapes that could help you to learn some important techniques for your profession or perhaps a foreign language you want to brush up on—but haven't got around to getting it just yet. Maybe next week. . . . the list goes on.

True prioritizing takes into account the importance of the task to be completed and the urgency but never letting the former be at the mercy of the latter. There are times when urgency will be responded to, when you don't know what the priority is (as when the telephone rings). There are also times when such interruptions must be ignored or turned off in favor of an obviously more important task.

Part of the prioritizing process is weighing each project and task to determine which should get your urgent attention. *You* decide. *You* place the urgency. *You* take control and move the vital, must do, projects ahead.

4

Power Planning— The Productivity Pyramid

Every great personal victory was preceded by a personal goal or dream—a dream that sprang from the value core of some individual. All good behavior springs from good principles.

Dennis R. Webb

I've always been fascinated by the study of human behavior. I often wonder why people do what they do or why some individuals seem to have a knack for achievement—perhaps even driven to succeed in some venture or to support some cause they believe in strongly. Goals by themselves aren't the answer. Columbus didn't sit in a vacuum and decide to discover a new route to the Indies. The courage of Thomas More wasn't the result of momentary moral impulse. Martin Luther King's vision of social justice in America wasn't just a casual idea that came to him while reading the morning paper. Significantly, each of these men persisted in their actions at great personal loss. And yet, they took their stand, lived it, and eventually died for it. The idea that "every man has his price" is a shameful thought in light of such conduct.

The roots of their behavior, and ours, are the *principles* or *values* that drive conduct. It's zeal or fire, born of purpose—a basic understanding of what is important to us. Those who achieve the most, in spite of personal or public resistance, are very clear about what they stand for. Moreover, I believe that significant contribution in any endeavor is impossible without clarity on worthy values.

Some years ago, after researching a paper I was writing about human motivation, I reviewed the works of Abraham Maslow, particularly his famous "Hierarchy of Needs." It occurred to me that if I were to overlay Maslow's pyramid with the basic elements of goal achievement, using values as a base, I would have a simple model of value-based achievement. The idea went onto the back burner for several years. I did use it on several occasions, primarily to show subordinates how value-based goal setting worked. Then one day I was invited to attend a time management seminar taught by a friend. My friend, as a part of the seminar, was trying to show the continuity between values and goal setting. "Wow," I thought. "I've got a model that shows that relationship!" After some tinkering with the model, the Productivity Pyramid was "born."

The model has at its base the highest priorities of our personal lives or of our organization —Governing Values. When identified and expanded upon, these values provide the rules or principles guiding the goal-setting process. Long-range goals are then set within the framework of the Governing Values. Intermediate goals are then formulated, based on the long-range goals. Finally, the process culminates in a list of "daily tasks" or personal daily behavior.

For the remainder of this chapter we will be working our way up through the Productivity Pyramid, starting with Governing Values, moving through formal goal setting and ending at the "Productivity Point"—the daily task level. As we move along, you will be asked to review your highest priorities—your values—and to evaluate your daily behavior in light of the principles you identify. In chapter five, using these values as a base, you will write long-range goals that will be further refined into intermediate steps. Then, in chapter six, we will get specific about daily planning and the use of the Franklin Day Planner.

Of all the chapters in this book, this single chapter will be the most significant for you *if* you follow the procedures outlined and implement your plan. If you sincerely apply the principles of the Productivity Pyramid you will magnify your control of events. You will become a master of time management.

At Franklin, we receive thousands of letters every month from seminar graduates. These letters report various amounts of progress in gaining control of events through applying the principles and techniques taught. Following is an excerpt from one such letter:

I completed my pyramid one week after the seminar. It was hard for me because I had to really think about my life and what was important to me. Now that I've completed that task I've come to realize that this was the most important part of the assignment (just like you said it would be!). Now, in my daily planning I sincerely consider my values and plan them into my daily tasks. The difference in what I accomplish each day is remarkable —and I feel so good about it! Thanks.

GOVERNING VALUES

Valuing is a process of crystallizing your highest priorities into a set of value statements. These value statements then provide the basis for goal setting.

I first became aware of value-based goal setting when studying the work of Paul J. Meyer, president of the Success Motivation Institute. In his goal-setting module, Meyer had his students evaluate the key values of their lives in preparation for setting personal goals. He writes:

A program of goal-setting always implies the existence of a system of values. Two otherwise very desirable goals may conflict with each other. Knowing where you stand includes not only knowing what you think, believe and do, but also knowing which beliefs are the strongest.

Emerson said, ''Nothing gives so much direction to a person's life as a set of sound principles.'' Identifying personal values is a way of revealing these important principles (values) to ourselves.

THE FRANKLIN METHOD

In history there are many exemplary people who achieved greatness in their lives and thereby made contributions that have benefited the world. Likewise there are many today on similar quests. The driving force in the lives of these people has always been an ideal of some kind—a value-based idea that drove them on and kept them to the task.

One of the most successful people who ever lived was Benjamin Franklin. Although of extremely humble beginnings, Franklin rose to be one of the most successful and respected men in the American colonies—a man of awesome scope and accomplishment. National defense, the national post office, the public library, and the University of Pennsylvania all were initiated by Franklin. Franklin's inventions and experiments are known to nearly every school child—or should be. To read Franklin's autobiography is to be drawn to him as he tells honestly and sweetly about his family, friends, and faults—all within ''earshot'' of accounts of governors, merchants, Indians, and kings.

By 1728, Franklin had moved (actually run away) from his birthplace in Boston, Massachusetts, to Philadelphia, Pennsylvania, where he had worked for various printers. By then he was part owner of a print shop. In 1730, two years later, be became the sole owner of the business and began publishing *The Pennsylvania Gazette*. His name gradually became known throughout the colonies because of the success of his business. He believed that in order to be successful in business, one had to simply work harder than one's competitors. And he did. One of his neighbors once said, ''The industry of that Franklin is superior to anything I ever saw . . . I see him still at work when I go home from club; and he is at work again before his neighbors are out of bed.''

To quote Franklin: ''It was about this time I conceiv'd the bold and arduous project of arriving at moral perfection. I wished to live without committing any fault at any time; I would conquer all that either natural inclination, custom, or company might lead me into. As I knew, or thought I knew, what was right and wrong, I did not see why I might not always do the one and avoid the other.'' With this statement, Franklin begins the account of his most remarkable achievements and gives us a step-by-step formula to follow.

The first step Franklin took was to list and prioritize all the values (he referred to them as virtues) in his life that he wanted to perfect. Then, in order to define the action which should be associated with each value, he ''annex'd to each a short precept, which fully express'd the extent I gave to its meaning.'' In other words, he described for himself behavior that would be ideal—within the framework of the value. Here are Franklin's virtues:

- *Temperance.* Eat not to dullness; drink not to elevation.
- *Silence.* Speak not but what may benefit others or yourself; avoid trifling conversation.
- *Order.* Let all your things have their places; let each part of your business have its time.
- *Resolution.* Resolve to perform what you ought; perform without fail what you resolve.
- *Frugality.* Make no expense but to do good to others or yourself; that is, waste nothing.
- *Industry.* Lose no time; be always employed in something useful; cut off all unnecessary actions.
- *Sincerity.* Use no hurtful deceit; think innocently and justly; speak accordingly.
- *Justice.* Wrong none by doing injuries; or omitting the benefits that are your duty.
- *Moderation.* Avoid extremes; forbear resenting injuries so much as you think you deserve.
- *Cleanliness.* Tolerate no uncleanliness in body, clothes, or habitation.
- *Tranquility.* Be not disturbed at trifles or at accidents common or unavoidable.

- *Chastity.* Rarely use venery but for health or offspring, never to dullness, weakness, or the injury of your own or another's peace or reputation.
- *Humility.* Imitate Jesus and Socrates.

At first, Franklin thought he could simply refer to these values and their behavior statements periodically and be sufficiently reminded of his goal. He quickly found out that such a casual approach wouldn't do. "I soon found I had undertaken a task of more difficulty than I had imagined. While my care was employ'd in guarding against one fault, I was often surprised by another; habit took the advantage of inattention; inclination was sometimes too strong for reason."

Realizing after short experiment that "daily examination would be necessary," Franklin "contrived the following method for conducting that examination. I made a little book, in which I allotted a page for each of the virtues. I rul'd each page with red ink, so as to have seven columns, one for each day, marking each column with a letter for the day. I cross'd these columns with thirteen red lines, marking the beginning of each line with the first letter of one of the virtues."

Once his "little book" was designed and completed, Franklin kept daily account of his progress toward his goal—marking each distraction from progress by a small black spot. His ideal was to complete a day, then a week, etc., with no black spots.

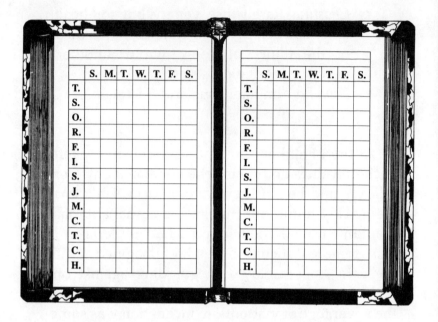

	S.	M.	T.	W.	T.	F.	S.
T.							
S.							
O.							
R.							
F.							
I.							
S.							
J.							
M.							
C.							
T.							
C.							
H.							

Franklin continued to refine his methods and techniques throughout his life. However, as he contrived each day's activities he always began with the question "What good shall I do this day?" and ended each day with "What good have I done today?" Under the virtue of Order, he expanded this idea to include a daily planning regimen where he formulated his daily tasks (which always included personal study) and made a daily resolution. His "little book" was used as a guide for both remembering his commitments and also to track his progress.

Writing in his autobiography at the age of seventy-nine, Franklin records:

I entered upon the execution of this plan for self-examination and continu'd it, with occasional intermissions for some time. . . . but I always carried my little book with me. . . . And it may be well my posterity should be informed that to his little artifice (his little book), with the blessing of God, their ancestor owed the constant felicity of his life down to his 79th year in which this is written. I hope, therefore, that some of my descendants may follow the example and reap the benefit.

IDENTIFYING YOUR VALUES

Using Benjamin Franklin's method, begin to evaluate the highest priorities of *your* life, your personal values. What are the most important things to you? If you 'boil out' all the relative trivialities of your life and get down to the bedrock of your existence, what do you find? This is obviously a personal, introspective process—you are looking inward at yourself.

The values you identify and describe will, of course, be unique to you. However, you may find some commonality with the values of others. The list below contains a number of value examples. This list isn't meant to be an exhaustive check list, but rather an idea starter. These are the types of things I mean when I use the term Governing Value:

- I am productive
- I am teachable
- I am innovative
- I encourage justice
- I love my family
- I serve others
- I am frugal
- I am a leader
- I love God

- I am self-sufficient
- I seek truth
- I am honest
- I am generous
- I have integrity
- I grow intellectually
- I am financially secure
- I am physically fit
- I am competent

Remember, the preceding list is not an inventory of possible values but rather a list of some commonly identified values. Also, notice that these value statements are written as affirmations. Affirmations, according to Webster, are "the act of asserting, or confirming as true, a positive assertion." Others have defined affirmations as "self-suggestion" or self-talk," "self-commands," or "self-motivators." Affirmations are positive declarations of what we believe and desire to live by. Here, I am simply trying to use the most powerful statements possible to get us started and to help us follow through on our plan.

Using a pad of paper and a pencil, write down the values you would identify for yourself. Write them as affirmations if you can. However, the important thing is to get your value thoughts down on paper. There is no hard and fast rule here, but in my experience most people are able to identify between six and twenty discreet values for themselves. How many you end up with depends on how you choose to word them and how many you combine. Also, some refining will naturally take place later when you add, subtract, or change written value statements.

Once you have your values identified, consider which ones have the highest value for you. Some will obviously emerge as more important, or more pressing. See if you can find one value that you consider your number one. Then, find number two, and three, etc. The idea here is to order your values into some kind of sequence representing priority.

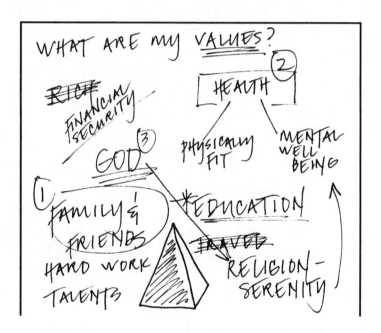

Once your values are identified and prioritized, you will want to clarify each value further by writing statements beneath each one that describes your *ideal* behavior as it relates to that value. For example, suppose you identified health as a high priority value. You might have written your value statement as:

I am physically healthy.

You could begin by asking yourself the question "If I were living that value perfectly, what would my behavior be like?" Or you could simply describe the most desirable behavior you can think of that relates to your value statement. Perhaps you could ask "What does a person do or not do if they really want to be healthy?" Write down your thoughts and ideas.

Once you're satisfied with your list of ideas, you can write them as your specific ideal behavior statements under your value name.

I maintain good health habits—diet,
exercise, and rest. I avoid habits that do not
contribute to good health.

You complete the value exercise by going through a similar process with each of your identified values. Below is a completed list of example value statements for your reference, as needed.

I am self-reliant. My finances are in order. I have sufficient supplies of necessities to meet my needs.

I am an outstanding parent. I plan and spend quality one-on-one time with each family member. I build the self-esteem of each person in my family. I help plan family activities which encourage togetherness and a supportive, loving atmosphere.

I strive for excellence. I do my best at every vital task and foster a standard of excellence in others.

The personal list of value statements you develop are a vital part of the planning process that will follow as you build your pyramid. I strongly urge you to formalize your list and review your values often. These statements represent your highest priorities and they will serve you well if you keep them in remembrance.

ORGANIZATIONAL VALUES

Many corporations, organizations, and associations have discovered the power of having a set of values that provide essential underpinnings to policy and goal planning. Such published statements of purpose can have a galvanizing effect on employee behavior. An employee who has internalized the idea that the company she works for "stands for quality in workmanship" takes pride in making sure that the work that is within her influence meets that standard.

Thomas Watson, Jr., once wrote a book about values in business titled *A Business and Its Beliefs*. In it, he makes this statement:

I believe the real difference between success and failure in a corporation can very often be traced to the question of how well the organization brings out the great energies and talents of its people. What does it do to help these people find common cause with each other? . . . I firmly believe that any organization, in order to survive and achieve success, must have a sound set of beliefs on which it premises all its policies and actions. Next, I believe that the most important single factor in corporate success is faithful adherence to those beliefs. And, finally, I believe if an organization is to meet the challenge of a changing world, it must be prepared to change everything about itself except those beliefs as it moves through corporate life. In other words, the basic philosophy, spirit, and drive of an organization have far more to do with its relative achievements than do technological or economic resources, organization structure, innovation, and timing. All these things weigh heavily in success. But they are, I think, transcended by how strongly the people in the organization believe in its basic precepts and how faithfully they carry them out.

There is interesting insight to be gained from this idea of corporate or organizational values. What Benjamin Franklin discovered in his quest for "moral perfection" is a true principle of achievement. Like all true principles, the application is not one dimensional. It works for individuals and organizations alike. It also will work for scout troops, church groups, soldiers, ball teams, etc.

Several years ago a very popular and poignant movie titled *Lean On Me* was produced which related the true story of an inner-city school in Philadelphia. The school had become dysfunctional because of the effects of drugs and other distractions from educational purposes. Academic halls had become a war zone where gangs of unruly students victimized students and teachers alike. The obvious result was an extremely high drop-out rate and an extremely low academic achievement from the students who stayed.

A new principal was assigned to the school to "clean up the mess"—and he did. He did it by first throwing out, by force, all those students who were in school to disrupt and prey on others, by recommitting the teacher corps, then by giving the student body some values and goals to live by. Over time, these values and associated objectives became the philosophy and spirit that drove good, sound, academic behaviors.

FAMILY VALUES

One cold winter day I spoke to a convention of dentists in Minneapolis, Minnesota. During my presentation I talked a good deal about personal values and how, if documented and used in goal setting, they could accelerate achievement and positive behavior change. After my talk, a woman approached me with this question, "Could this idea of values work in a family?" I really hadn't considered it before, but I felt confident that it would work so I said so and asked her to let me know what happened.

Several months later I got a letter from her telling me about her experiences. As it turned out, she had three sons—all teenagers. She never mentioned a husband so I assume she was either divorced or widowed. She told me that she sat with her three sons and explained to them the process I had outlined. They then decided what their family values were and particularly how they, as family members, would relate to each other in their home. After a lively discussion, they wrote out a family "constitution" and hung it on the family room wall.

She explained that an interesting change came about in their home. Her sons got along better—more cooperation and less fighting. When a behavioral problem did occur, a quick visit to the family room "constitution" and a review of the agreed-to principles usually corrected the problem. She said, "One real advantage to me was that I didn't have to be the policeman in my home anymore—our constitution became the agent of discipline." Imagine that.

Most of us remember Benjamin Franklin for his experiments with electricity—the kite and key thing. Or, maybe we are aware of his inventing the

Franklin stove, the lightning rod, bifocal eye-glasses, or any number of other useful, society-centered conveniences. To me it is important to know why and how he accomplished his great works so we can follow. Franklin, led as he was by a lifelong concern for the happiness, well-being, and dignity of humanity, gave us his most precious gift by his example.

Once our personal values are in order we, like Franklin, are ready to decide what specific contributions we will make. We're now ready to apply principles of goal setting.

5

Goals and Goal Setting

If you really know what things you want out of life, it's amazing how opportunities will come to enable you to carry them out.

John M. Goddard

Once you have completed your personal Governing Values and know where you stand with respect to your ideal, you are ready to formulate a plan of action—determining and writing your goals. When I use the term "goal setting" I am simply referring to a planning process—a process of controlling events that are in the future.

A GOAL IS A PLANNED-FOR EVENT

Someone has said that a goal is "a dream with a deadline." I like that. Goal setting ought to be invigorating and exciting to us—it's the beginning step toward reaching our dreams. Dreaming is imagining or visualizing some thing or some condition that doesn't exist now for us, but one we would like to exist very much. Goal setting is getting specific with dreams— bringing them into a format where we can begin to work toward them and ultimately realize them.

A few years ago a nationwide survey was conducted in America about goal setting. Results of the study showed that only about 3 percent of people surveyed had written plans or goals for life. An additional 10 percent had goals or a fairly good idea about their life objectives but hadn't written them down. Another 60 percent had some idea of what they needed financially to retire in some reasonable fashion but that was about it. Over 25 percent hadn't given any real thought to goals or future planning at all. Interestingly, 3 percent were considered highly successful, 10 percent were considered comfortable, 60 percent were of modest means and about 30 percent were struggling in life.

My grandfather used to say, "Be careful what you aim for; you might hit it." It's a true principle. Serious goal setting produces serious results.

Our minds are naturally goal seeking. Our minds, conscious and subconscious, are constantly looking for direction from us. Given clear, specific direction, our minds help us to concentrate our energies on and open our eyes to opportunities to express our desires. People who have no clear direction and who seem to wander from one job or task to another don't get much done of any value.

Goal setting, long-range and intermediate, represents the second and third level of the Productivity Pyramid.

FOUR KEY ELEMENTS OF GOAL SETTING

Before writing goals, we should review some key elements of well-worded goal statements. First, it is vitally important that you write your

goals down. Written goals provide a needed yard-
stick with which to gauge progress. Also, the act of
writing goals lends dedication and purpose to
achievement. Finally, periodic review of our goals
gives an added boost when our memories become
lazy or motivation ebbs. Goals should be:

1. *Supported by Governing Values*
   The value statements written in the value identification exercise should serve as a guide for certain
goals. For example, if you have identified the value
''I will maintain excellent health'' and yet your behavior suggests that you are neglecting your health
in some way, you will want to set some specific
goals to bring your behavior in line with your
value. In other instances, you may want to simply
make sure your goals or the method used to reach
them are not in conflict with your Governing
Values.

2. *Clearly and Specifically Written*
   Goal statements should be written in such a
way as to clearly define the future event. Being specific is important because it helps to crystallize our
thinking. Psychologists tell us that the commitment
to a clearly written goal is three times as high as the
commitment to an unclear goal or one we only
carry in our heads.

3. *Measurable or Time Dimensioned*
   Goals should have deadlines. Deadlines act on
us by providing urgency to action. Deadlines fix

our minds on a future date-target. Deadlines are the "firing pin" of goal achievement. Other measurable data should also be included—how many pounds are you going to lose? How much savings will you accumulate? Which graduate school will you attend?

4. *Personal and Attainable*

We should "own" our goals. Not that they must be unique, but we should internalize them—they must be ours. Goals should also be clearly attainable. They should make us reach, stretch, and change, but they should be within our grasp. To set a goal that is unattainable is to defeat ourselves before we start.

LONG-RANGE GOALS

The second level of the Productivity Pyramid relates to those goals that are our ultimate objective. Long-range goals, by definition, are not "half-steps" to some other, longer range goal. Whether the goal is twenty days into the future or twenty years depends on the nature of the goal itself. It also may depend somewhat on the experience of the goal setter. Typically, when first learning how to set goals, shorter long-range goals work best—they build confidence in ability in the same way a golfer gains confidence in putting, learning how to make the short (three foot) putts first, building confidence for the longer putts later on.

SOMEDAY I'M GOING TO

It is a fact that each of us has a number of things "left undone" in our lives. These things are future events for us that are still in the dream phase. Things we're going to do—someday. We have a pretty good idea about the desired end result, but we haven't taken the time to get specific, either in defining the goal or giving it that all-important deadline. In seminars I commonly ask the question of seminar participants, "What are you going to do someday?" I get a variety of answers.

"Someday I'm going to:

- Get a college degree
- Learn to speak a foreign language

- Build a log cabin
- Learn to do calligraphy
- Get a better job
- Visit Hawaii
- Get my pilots license
- Go to Europe

Let me try to put some urgency on your goal setting. I'd like you to consider for a moment a Time Line. You've probably seen historical time lines, showing dates and events as they occurred in relation to one another. Time lines are typified by having a beginning and an end with events pinpointed along the line as illustrated.

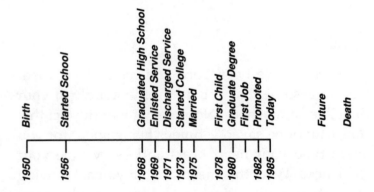

The time line I'd like you to ponder now is your own. Your time line has a beginning event (birth) and an ending event (death). You can write down your birthdate— it's a matter of record, and you probably take it for granted, but it's a rather significant date for you. You also have a death date. You don't know when it is, but you know it's out there as a future event somewhere.

●────────────────────────────────●
(BIRTH)   **(DEATH)**

Since you've been born and haven't yet died, we can assume that you are in the middle of your time line somewhere. Now, remember the fact that time cannot be saved —time is being spent for you every time your heart beats and every time your clock ticks. What this means is that you are moving through your time line toward your death, every single second—you can't stop yourself!

It is significant that those events you may have thought about as Someday I'm going to's are moving through the time line at exactly the same rate of speed you are. In other words, you're not getting any closer to them.

Well, I can't do much about your death date. You can, perhaps, by being more aware and making necessary and appropriate life-style changes to lengthen out your life. But the fact remains that none of us is going to get out of this life alive. What you *can do* is plan for some of your vital long-range goals as if you mean it! Then you can work toward having a life full of achievement and fulfillment. Now that's living!

Think of your time line again. Imagine your future filled with realizations of your most important dreams. Only this time, your somedays have specific dates and are defined in specific measurable terms. Now your goals don't float along with you—they're fixed in place on your time line. You, however, *are* moving through the time line and reaching your goals now becomes a matter of event control—a matter of time management.

GOAL CATEGORIES

Getting started in goal setting is much like learning any new skill—sometimes it helps to have examples and obvious places to start. The categories listed below are designed to get you thinking about setting goals across a broad spectrum of your life. The idea is to underscore the need to achieve a sense of balance, and particularly to start your goal setting in an area that needs the most attention. These categories have been selected because they represent the most common areas of goal setting. You may want to add a few categories of your own.

- Physical well-being
- Family
- Spiritual/humanitarian
- Financial
- Company—career
- Company—strategic
- Community/political
- Educational/personal development

As you review the list are there categories that give your conscience a pang? Feeling a little guilt? It is not uncommon for each of us to recognize an area of our lives that has suffered neglect. If you felt any such feelings, perhaps that is an indication of where you should start your personal goal setting.

Below is a brief series of self-evaluating questions you may want ask yourself as you prepare for some personal goal setting. These may serve as idea starters for your own goals.

Physical
- Have I had a complete medical/dental examination in the last year?
- Am I involved in a systematic program of physical exercise?

- Am I at my optimum weight level for my height and build?
- Do I have any harmful habits that need control?

Family
- Am I spending enough time with my family?
- Do I spend one-on-one time with each of my children?
- Do I help plan meaningful family activities?
- Have we had or are we planning a family vacation?
- Do I take business work home frequently?

Spiritual/humanitarian
- Have I volunteered to help another in need lately?
- Am I living my moral and ethical principles?
- Should I attend church more often?
- Do I foster a teachable, humble attitude?

Company/career
- Do I have a plan for career advancement?
- Do I understand my next career step and how to get there?
- Have I communicated my expectations to my boss?
- Will my current career path get me where I want to go?

Company/strategic

- Do I have specific production/sales goals?
- Do my projects get finished on time and within budget?
- How can I be more effective on the job?
- Am I building my subordinates?

Financial

- Am I living within my income?
- Do I have an ongoing savings or investment plan?
- Will I have the money I need to retire as I want to?
- Am I using credit wisely?

Community/political

- Am I aware of and helping to solve community problems?
- Do I actively support my political party?
- Am I engaged in good community causes?
- Are my neighbors known to me and I to them?

Educational/personal development

- Is my education and training well rounded?
- Do I have a reading list of subjects to learn about?
- Have I been to the theater/art show/concert lately?
- Have I planned time for rest and recreation?

These questions are designed to get your thinking started and to test your emotional response to each category. Perhaps you felt at ease with certain ones and ill at ease with others. Because there may be a higher level of urgency to work on a category that makes you feel the least comfortable, start with the category that, according to your conscience, needs the most attention.

Suppose you feel the need to begin your goal setting in the educational/personal development category. You'll want to select a future condition that you would like to exist for yourself in this area—perhaps you already have a very specific idea. Whether you pick a goal idea that is two or three years away or one that is next month will have something to do with the amount of confidence you feel toward the task.

Here's an example:

GOAL PLANNING

VALUES & GOALS

VALUE: _____

| Daily Task List |
| Intermediate Goals |
| Long-Range Goals |
| Values |

LONG RANGE GOAL:

IN THREE YEARS, I WILL HAVE
COMPLETED A COLLEGE LEVEL
COURSE IN BEGINNING FRENCH
AT CITY UNIVERSITY.

Priority	Intermediate Goals (Daily Tasks)	Deadlines

Notice that the written goal is specific in describing the end result. It also has a deadline. It meets all the criteria and is a well-written goal.

Obviously there are many things that will need to happen in order for this future event to be realized. These "things" are called "Intermediate Goals."

INTERMEDIATE GOALS

Because our long-range goals cannot be completed in a day, it is necessary to reduce them to short-range, intermediate steps. In doing so, we

are moving up the Productivity Pyramid and coming a little closer to reaching our objectives. The rules for or keys to writing intermediate goal statements are the same as those for long-range goals. However, as we move up the pyramid our goals become more measurable and more specific.

Using the preceding long-range goal we wrote, let's establish intermediate goals that will give greater direction to our effort. First you will want to consider all the things that will need to happen in order to reach your goal. For example: When do the next French classes begin at City University? Do you need a course catalog to determine the best timing/location? What will be the cost? How will you prepare financially? Will you need to rearrange your schedule? Write your answers or identified intermediate steps on a piece of paper and get them organized by sequence.

If you have a family to care for or if you live many miles from the university, or if other complications may be involved, your goal planning will need to take all these things into account. Don't be discouraged at this point if it seems too complex. Make appropriate adaptations as necessary, but stay focused on your goal.

Once you have an organized list, write the steps on your goal planning form in order of sequence. Don't forget your deadlines!

The intermediate goals are your "road map" to the long-range objective. They should give you encouragement and reinforce your desire for the condition stated in your ultimate objective. Notice how

GOAL PLANNING

VALUES & GOALS

VALUE: _____

_____

_____

(pyramid diagram: Daily Task List / Intermediate Goals / Long-Range Goals / Values)

LONG RANGE GOAL:

IN THREE YEARS I WILL HAVE
COMPLETED A COLLEGE LEVEL
COURSE IN BEGINNING FRENCH
AT CITY UNIVERSITY.

Priority	Intermediate Goals (Daily Tasks)	Deadlines
	GET A COURSE CATALOG	OCT. 2, '92
	SELECT COURSE SCHEDULE	OCT. 9, '92
	ENROLL IN CLASS	NOV. 1, '92
	SCHEDULE CLASS NIGHTS	DEC. 7, '92
	MAKE ARRANGEMENT FOR SITTER	DEC. 10 '92
	TUITION PAYMENT	JAN. 4, '93
	BEGIN CLASSES	JAN. 6, '93

simple the short-range goals look? As these milestones are determined and written, you will begin to visualize more clearly the reaching of your goal. *N'est-ce pas?*

OVERCOMING OBSTACLES

As goals are broken down into smaller elements they look simpler and more easily attainable. That's good. It helps build excitement and anticipation. However, obstacles will present themselves. If you ask yourself the question, "What things could get in my way in reaching this goal?" you may be forced to consider some real possibilities. Then, if you think of something significant, ask yourself, "What can I do to overcome this problem?" In a mystical way that I don't fully understand, answers come—simply, easily, accurately. The solutions to obstacles are usually within ourselves. Part of gaining control of events is planning for the unforeseen.

For most people the biggest obstacle is their own habits. Even simple changes in behavior are hard to make. We have established "Comfort Zones" for ourselves that are hard to break out of. James W. Newman, author of *Release Your Brakes!*, is the creator of the concept of comfort zones. In his book he teaches that we all have a tendency to move toward our comfort zones, and to stay in them.

We all have places and conditions where we feel at ease and comfortable. We also have comfort levels with *things*. For example, we have "comfort clothes" and "comfort food." (That's why we eat our own food at potluck dinners!) The process of making progress and changing our behavior requires us to leave, and thereby expand the perimeter or even create new comfort zones for ourselves.

Actually, leaving one's comfort zone to reach important personal goals should be an invigorating, exciting experience. Newman likens this experience to an "adventure." He says, "Adventure is the deliberate volitional movement out of one's comfort zone."

The adventure of reaching our goals ought to be a daily one. Each day we should be progressing, learning, striving, and improving ourselves. Once our intermediate goals are determined, our next step is to plan for this daily adventure.

6

The Power in Today

*You have to live on this twenty-four hours of daily time.
Out of it you have to spin wealth, pleasure, money, content, respect, and the evolution of your immortal soul. Its
right use is a matter of highest urgency . . . all depends
on that.*

Arnold Bennett

It is a fact that we accomplish our tasks on a
daily basis, not weekly or monthly or yearly. It is
our daily strategy that moves us toward our goals
and objectives. As we have pointed out in the prior
chapter, it is vital for us to have our long-range
goals and to have these broken down into intermediate goals in order that we may successfully reach

them. These long-range targets, however, are established to provide a perspective on today.

Ari Kiev, in his book *A Strategy for Daily Living*, writes, "A successful life does not result from chance nor is it determined by fate or good fortune, but from a succession of successful days." Kiev's thought, that we can have a successful day and combine it with another to make two and then ten and then a lifetime of days, is fundamental to achieving our goals.

Throughout this book we have been focusing on the essentials of successful time management. This process has included writing of goals and avoiding the common pitfalls which deter the pursuit of personal productivity. This final phase of the Productivity Pyramid is the key to maintaining control on a daily basis.

Most organized people will use, on a daily basis, several devices to help them stay "organized." These would probably include:

- An appointment calendar
- A daily "to do" list
- A pad for daily notes
- A phone/address book

When these tools are used appropriately, in concert with one another, they can help you to achieve a measure of control in your daily organization. We can enhance the process greatly if we have all of these essential items, and a few more, in one place, a "place" that moves through the day with us, providing focus and flexibility wherever we are.

THE FRANKLIN DAY PLANNER

When the Franklin International Institute was first formed we simply taught time management seminars—we didn't have a tool that met our exact needs for implementing the principles we taught. From our research, it was clear that Benjamin Franklin had designed a datebook that helped him to focus his energies on his daily priorities. In his autobiography he even gave a great deal of credit for his life's achievements to the fact that he carried his "little book" with him wherever he went. So we set out to find out what was available and, more specifically, to find out what we needed in order to enhance the ongoing effects of our seminar.

The result of this effort was the "Franklin Day Planner," first published in January of 1984. The Day Planner was the result of gleaning from available datebook/organizers of the day the ideas we thought were most useful. Then we designed sections that expanded or enhanced the utility of the tool for seminar participants. As this book goes to press, there are over a million Day Planner users throughout the world, proving once again that Benjamin Franklin's principles of time management are just as valid today as they were 260 years ago.

DAILY PLANNING PROCEDURE

In the example that follows, I will be suggesting a daily procedure for planning and organizing your day to maximum effectiveness using the Franklin Day Planner.

The Monthly Calendar Page

This page provides the user with a quick reference to the entire month. It should serve as the ''master'' calendar for the month and contain all appointments, scheduled events, important dates, etc.

A glance at this calendar will help you to see how the scheduled events fit together or how the month ''flows.'' Problem areas can be seen and prepared for in advance. Also, I find it useful to write all important anniversaries, birthdays, school holidays, etc., on these monthly pages for the entire year. Highlighting them with a colored marker helps me to recognize them in plenty of time to appropriately respond.

SEPTEMBER 1991

SUN.	MON.	TUES.	WED.	THURS.	FRI.	SAT.
1	**2** LABOR DAY LABOUR DAY (CANADA)	**3**	**4** 8 STAFF MTG.	**5**	**6** 9 BALL & HUNT MTG. 8-16	**7** 4 JULIE GAME
8 7 CHOIR PRACTICE	**9** FAMILY DINNER ROSH HASHANAH	**10** 10 IGM CHAMBERS	**11** U526 7:50 A.M. ARRIVE LAX 150	**12** REGIONAL MEETING HYATT REGENCY	**13** 10-11 D335 6:05	**14** ANGELA CALLS B-DAY
15 7 CHOIR PRACTICE	**16** 11 JOHN SANDERS LUNCH 6-3	**17** BOB WILLIAMS 12-5 YOM KIPPUR	**18** 8 STAFF MTG.	**19** 1 PROJ. MTG 8-15	**20** DICKS B-DAY	**21** SKIING @ NOLAN'S LODGE W/JONES
22 7 CHOIR PRACTICE	**23** 10 BILL BERNER 9-4	**24**	**25**	**26**	**27** ROTARY LUNCH SYMPHONY	**28**
29	**30** MOM'S BIRTHDAY					

28

SATURDAY
SEPTEMBER 28
1991

S	M	T	W	T	F	S
1	2	3	4	5	6	7
8	9	10	11	12	13	14
15	16	17	18	19	20	21
22	23	24	25	26	27	**28**
29	30					

↙ = Task Completed
→ = Planned Forward
x = Task Deleted
G⊘ = Delegated Task
● = In Process

AUGUST 1991

S	M	T	W	T	F	S
				1	2	3
4	5	6	7	8	9	10
11	12	13	14	15	16	17
18	19	20	21	22	23	24
25	26	27	28	29	30	31

OCTOBER 1991

S	M	T	W	T	F	S
		1	2	3	4	5
6	7	8	9	10	11	12
13	14	15	16	17	18	19
20	21	22	23	24	25	26
27	28	29	30	31		

PRIORITIZED DAILY TASK LIST

✓	ABC Priority	
✓	A1	PLANNING
✓	A4	READING 20 MINUTES
✓	B2	SEE ANDREW RE: MTG
→	C3	OUTLINE TRIP REPORT
✓	B1	CALL NANCY RE: 8-17
✓	A3	WRITE TO KORING INC.
→	C2	CLEAR IN-DRAWER
✓	B3	SEND IMPACT MEMO TO ALL
✓	A2	GET APPL' FOR PROJECT
✓	C1	DO EXPENSE SUMMARY
✓	*	VERIFY LUNCH/HARRIS
→	C1	CLEAN HALL CLOSET
✓	A1	CALL MOM RE: DINNER (14)
✓	B2	PICK UP TICKETS
→	B1	TAKE IN DRY CLEANING

DAILY EXPENSES

LUNCH W/ HENDERSON	$9.85
PARKING	1.50

APPOINTMENT SCHEDULE

Early Morning

8 STAFF MEETING

9

10

11 LUNCH
BEN HENDERSON
12 HARRIS SHIPPING
@ HYATT

1

2 PROD. COMMITTEE
MTG. - CONF 4

3

4

5

6

7 NORTH CREEK HOME
OWNERS MTG.
8 CLARKS HOME

Late Evening

Daily Planning Page

This page will contain the daily schedule of appointments, your daily task list, and a place for recording any out-of-pocket expenses. Notice that it also includes small monthly reference calendars and a legend of important symbols.

In the next example notice the sample daily task list area. The tasks listed in this column should be broken down into small steps of fifteen to thirty minutes if possible. Such rendering will help you to avoid the natural tendency to procrastinate large tasks. Also, the number of tasks on your daily task list should be a function of how much *discretionary* time you have available in the day. A glance at your appointment schedule should give you a feel for how much freedom you have today and how many tasks you can reasonably accomplish with it.

Another handy idea is to separate the "personal" from the "business" tasks. Notice in the example that the personal tasks are listed below the others. Also, the priorities for personal tasks are entered in lowercase letters, indicating a separate prioritizing scheme.

• Commitments Exchanged
• Journal Entry
• Thoughts & Ideas
• Agendas (telephone, meetings)
• Conversations

SEPTEMBER 1991
DAILY RECORD OF EVENTS

28
SATURDAY
271st Day   94 Left
Week 39

① STAFF MEETING
  a. STEPHANIE SUGGESTED NEW PROCEDURE
    FOR HANDLING PETTY CASH.
  b. ALL INFORMED OF EXPENSE REDUCTION
    PLAN. ALL CONCUR.
  C. NEXT MEETING SCHED. FOR 12-6

② HARRIS SHIPPING - BEN HENDERSON
  a. WANTS FORMAL PROPOSAL
  b. DEMO SET FOR 12-14 @ 10:AM
  C. MENTIONED DISLIKE OF PAUL'S
    ATTITUDE @ FIRST MTG - SEE PAUL!

③ SANDY JONES - ACCOUNTING A/P
  WANTS DETAILS ON DEC. SUMMARY
  MEETING SET FOR THURS.

④ PROD. COMMITTEE MTG. - WES TAYLOR
  a. B - PHASE PROTOTYPE ON SCHED.
  b. INVENTORY OF ALUM. BACK PLATES
    IN QUESTION

⑤ BETTY WISE - ACCENT ON TRAVEL
  a. OPENING NEW OFFICE IN S.W. CTR.
  b. WANTS TO SPEAK @ ROTARY
  C. SHARP AND PROFESSIONAL -
    SEE LARRY

—— TALKED WITH JULIE TONITE RE:
BASKETBALL ETAL.
SHE WANTS TO MAKE THE TEAM
AND IS PRACTICING.

⑥ HOMEOWNERS MTG. RESCHEDULED
FOR FEB. 7 7?m @ BANTAS

Daily Record of Events Page

As you progress through your day, information important to you and your tasks will flow to you and from you for various reasons. I suggest you capture this information by taking simple reference notes on this page. Headings can separate notes and thoughts for easy retrieval. Since this is a daily record, your monthly calendar serves as a handy index to the recorded information. For days when many notes are necessary, additional pages can be added easily via nondated Daily Record of Events pages in the ring binder.

SEPTEMBER 1991
MASTER TASK LIST

PERSONAL	BUSINESS
O FAMILY ———	O COMPANY TASKS ——
PLAN SPRING VACATION	COMPLETE BUDGET
✓ BIRTHDAY GIFT FOR MOM	GET SEA. MAILER OUT
✓ INTERVIEW JULIE	✓ DO SALES MANUAL
TAKE KIDS TO ZOO	CALL ESI RE: PROJECT
	REVIEW AGENT CONTRACT
	✓ CHICAGO STUDY REVIEW
O PERSONAL ———	DO NEWSLETTER FORMAT
READ "HIGH OUTPUT MGM"	INTERVIEW STAN BROWN
RUN 2 MILES PER DAY	✓ DO PDR FOR SALLY
REG. FOR MGM 350	✓ CLEAR C DRAWER
FINISH GOALS FOR '91	✓ GET VACATION SCHED.
BUY NIKES T2005Z	CANCEL SUBSCRIPTION
	TO SC
O HOME ———	MEMO RE: CALENDARS
FIX B.YARD FENCE	✓ FINISH TIME LOG REVIEW
✓ PAINT FAMILY ROOM	PROPOSE PROD. STUDY
CLEAN HALL CLOSET	
CHANGE OIL IN CAR	
FEED LAWN	
✓ WRAP BSMT. PIPES	
O MISC. ———	
CALL LARRY SMITH	
CALL NATIONWIDE INS.	
MONTHLY GOALS	**MONTHLY GOALS**
	O TRIP PLANNING:
	✓ GET PASSPORT APPL.
	FINISH FRENCH LESSONS
	✓ BABYSITTER CONTRACTED
	PICK UP E. SHAVER
	✓ FLIGHT ARRANGEMTS.

The Master Task List

In the Franklin Day Planner, the Master Task List is located on the reverse of the Monthly Calendar. This list is simply a place to keep unassigned tasks until the time can be allotted for them. Consider it a dynamic monthly "to-do" list.

I have found it valuable to segment my personal Master Task List into categories as in the example shown. This way, each important aspect of my time will receive its proper emphasis.

Note: The Master Task List should be a repository for any tasks that cannot be assigned to a specific date. Consequently, during the daily planning period, you should review the Master Task List items to see if any might appropriately be added to today's Daily Task List. If you can apply a date to a task, the task should be entered into the Daily Task List for that future date.

As you do your daily planning and use your datebook/organizer, I suggest you consider the following general procedure. Like any new idea, this one may seem a little awkward at first, but when habitualized, it can be done with dispatch. The return on investment, in terms of your personal productivity, will be significant.

ENVIRONMENT FOR PLANNING

When you do your daily planning, I suggest you find a place where you may be free from distractions until you are finished with the process. If you arrive early or can stay late, your workspace is a likely spot. However, if you are accustomed to a high level of interruptions at your workspace, find another location for your planning period. Many find that a few extra minutes before leaving home is the best time for establishing the daily plan.

Incidentally, many people have asked me when is the best time to do daily planning—morning or evening. There is no set answer. I strongly feel that the late afternoon or just prior to leaving the office or workspace is the best time to plan the activities for the next day. Important events are still in mind and it is also a good time to review the events of your evening—making a clean break between work and personal life. However, most people find the morning the most agreeable time to plan and have made it a matter of habit to do so. The answer is up to the individual. The important thing is to *do* the planning every day.

REVIEW OF GOALS AND VALUES

Taking a few moments to review goals and values will provide needed direction to the day. As has been pointed out, it is too easy to get involved with relative trivialities and not focus on the things that matter most. Making sure that you plan for each day brings you a little closer to reaching your long-range objectives in your professional life and your personal life.

REVIEW TODAY'S SCHEDULE

Take a look at today's schedule. How many meetings or other appointments are scheduled in your day? How much time is available for your creative work and project responsibilities? The number of items on your daily task list will be determined by the amount of discretionary time available today.

REVIEW WEEKLY SCHEDULE

A quick glance at the week ahead will alert you to events that may need some preparation today. Also, with the rest of the week in mind, you may see blocks of uncommitted time available for project work that relates to today or, more important, you may see a time problem in advance that will affect today's plan.

REVIEW YOUR MASTER TASK LIST

Read through your Master Task List with an eye toward finding specific unassigned tasks that may appropriately be done today. If you find one or two that fit, add them to your daily task list. If not, the list will wait until tomorrow.

REVIEW PRIOR DAY'S TASK LIST

If you have uncompleted tasks from your prior day's list, plan them forward into today's list, a future daily task list or even your Master Task List.

PRIORITIZE DAILY TASKS

Once your daily plan is listed and prioritized, you will follow the procedures of your day, focusing on your plan periodically and making appropriate checks and notes. It is important to be flexible in your approach. As has been pointed out, many of us are interrupted often during the day. Even the best-laid plans need revision or sometimes need to be completely abandoned because of a major, unexpected problem. Remember to adapt to those things that are beyond your control.

It has been suggested that the key to success in time management is "plan your work and work your plan." Anyone with much experience in the business world, upon trying this principle, will deduce that the true axiom should be "plan your work—then, watch someone come along and mess it up."

Consider this. Even after applying the concepts of daily planning above, you may find yourself in a day that "ruins" your plan. Of the ten things you planned to do, you only accomplished four. However, the four things you did complete were the highest priority tasks for that day. You have then done your best under difficult circumstances. You have optimized control of events.

7

Time Flies— Where?

Effective Executives, in my observation, do not start with their tasks. They start with their time. They start by finding out where their time goes. Then they attempt to manage their time and to cut back unproductive demands on their time.

Peter F. Drucker

We've all been robbed of time. Sometimes the reason for the theft is obvious, other times the reason eludes us, suggesting a problem with deeper roots. As was mentioned in the prior chapter, our time is constantly being ''ripped-off'' by forces within and without. In our complex society, the demands on our time seem to increase yearly —role models in this society give suggestions that we should all be actively involved in advancing our respective careers, working for the betterment of the community, doing volunteer work in our political party, becoming a super parent, and coaching Little League or being a den mother. We mustn't forget to have a good daily exercise program, watch our diet, feed the dog, plant a garden, read a book, learn calligraphy, and take a course in self-defense. Is it any wonder that we sometimes feel victimized by the demands of the world around us? Is it any wonder that we belittle ourselves because we don't accomplish all that we could do?

It is true that no one has enough time to fulfill the expectations of everyone else. It is also true that everyone has been allotted exactly the same amount of time. Time, in a sense, is a great equalizer. When someone says there is or was not enough time, your response might appropriately be, "Not enough time?" "You've had all there is!" In truth, there is no more time (or any less, for that matter). Another fallacy concerning time is that it can be saved.

TIME CANNOT BE SAVED

Time must be spent. The spending of time, by the way, is something we have no control over. Time is spent for us—sixty seconds every minute, sixty minutes every hour. Because we cannot control the passing of time, we must be willing to readily adapt to the passage of time.

Since time cannot be saved, what then is the value of time management or event control? What each of us wants and enjoys most is the *discretion* to use our allotments of time as we want. That is why most people look forward to vacations, holidays, and weekends; blocks of time when we have obvious discretion over how we will spend time and, depending on our control level, we usually end up doing something we want to do. It is also true that most of us want discretion over how we spend our time on the job. We like to choose between alternatives and select our own course of action when we can. Fact is, we *need* discretionary time on a daily basis to accomplish important tasks at work and in our personal lives as well. Time-robbers steal this precious discretionary time and inhibit our quest for excellence.

TIME-ROBBERS

Who is robbing us of time? How is the theft taking place? What kind of control can we apply to overcome the problem? I have asked thousands of people to identify the major factors contributing to the theft of their time. If given a list, most can identify eight to twelve time-robbers that affect them frequently. Compiled below is a list of the most common time wasters identified by clients and seminar participants.

Evaluate your own time-robbers. Review the following lists and identify the time-robbers giving you the most difficulty. Since your goal is event control—ask yourself, "Which time-robbers are causing me to lose control?"

Time-Robbers

Group A	Group B
Interruptions	Failure to delegate
Waiting for answers	Poor attitude
Unclear job definition	Personal disorgani-
Unnecessary meetings	zation
Too much work	Absentmindedness
Poor communications	Failure to listen
Shifting priorities	Indecision
Equipment failure	Socializing
Disorganized boss	Fatigue
Red tape/procedures	Lack of self-discipline
Understaffed	Leaving tasks
Conflicting priorities	unfinished
Low company morale	Paper shuffling
Untrained staff	Procrastination
Peer/staff demands	Outside activities
Allowing upward	Cluttered workspace
delegation	Unclear personal goals
Inefficient office layout	Perfectionism
Interoffice travel	Poor planning
Mistakes of others	Attempting too much
	Preoccupation

Once you have identified those time-robbers that cause frequent control problems for you, go back over the list and find the time-robber that you think is causing you the greatest difficulty—your number one time-robber. When you find it, mark it with a number 1 and then find the numbers 2, 3, 4, and 5.

You probably noticed as you did your own time-robber test that the two groups of time-robbers above differ. Group A time-robbers are generally imposed by the environment of your work organization. Those in Group B are most often self-inflicted.

Review your top five time-robbers. Which ones were generated by you? Which ones were generated by environmental conditions? Thoughtfully consider your selections. What conditions caused the problem? To what extent were you an accomplice in environmental time robbing? Which ones could be eliminated? Which ones could be significantly reduced? While those time-robbers which were self-imposed are the easiest to identify a solution for, they are not necessarily the easiest to solve. Procrastination, lack of motivation, unclear objectives, etc., are recognizable as self-imposed time-robbers, but controlling these culprits will take time and effort. We will discuss each of these separately in later chapters. You may be interested in knowing how your selected time-robbers stack up against those most commonly selected by our time management seminar participants. Listed below are the time-robbers most often identified:

1. Interruptions
2. Procrastination
3. Shifting priorities
4. Poor planning
5. Waiting for answers

Also popular, but less so, are unnecessary meetings, conflicting priorities, poor communication, and unclear objectives. The time-robbers mentioned above have been compiled from seminars with many diverse groups across the nation. These groups have included financial consultants, auditors, engineers, secretaries, senior bank executives, homemakers, investment counselors, high school seniors, college students, government leaders, etc. The fascinating thing about these groups of people was how different their respective environments were but how similar their time-robbers were. Time-robbers don't seem to discriminate.

Did you know that you have habitualized your time-robbing? The ways that you wasted time today are much the same as the ways you wasted time last week and last month. In fact, unless you identify your principal time-robbers and implement a plan to reduce or eliminate them, you will continue wasting time in the same pattern.

Before you begin a detailed plan to control your time-robbers, let me ask you to consider another interesting fact about them. Evaluating a list and selecting a few areas of concern is really only the beginning of an appropriate, in-depth analysis. What you've identified in the above activity are areas you *think* are causing difficulty for you. You may be right, but most people aren't very precise about such self-analysis.

Wouldn't it be helpful if we had a little elf who could sit on our shoulder and go with us everywhere? As we engaged in our various activities and projects, our little elf would record our every move. Knowing us well and the priority of our tasks, our elf would record everything we did, how long it took us to complete and what the priority of the task or activity was. At the end of each two-week period, our little friend would present us with a well-formatted computer printout giving us detail and summary information on how we spent every minute. We'd really know what our time-robbers were then!

Of course, we don't have the resources of an elf as just described, but we do have the capacity to record daily time usage ourselves—and who better to do it? We are better able than anybody to assign priorities, understand our cryptic notes, and have insight to the variables associated with such an effort.

Do you know where your time actually goes? Do you have any idea *how many* interruptions you get each day or what level of priority they represent? How much time is available for creative thought? How much time *do you* spend in meetings?

These questions *can* be answered, but only after a detailed time-diagnosis. The idea is not to do a complex ''time and motion study'' on yourself, but rather to have a simple but effective way of recording key tasks and time slices in your day. Then, after you've accumulated enough significant data, you can personally do an analysis that can give you the information you need. The Franklin Time Log is designed to provide you with these advantages.

USING THE FRANKLIN TIME LOG

The first step in preparing to use a time log is a process of selecting the categories of time usage you would like to inventory and analyze. The time log I recommend is not the all-inclusive, two-hundred-category nightmare recording experience in use in many companies today, but rather a very simple tool for tracking those areas of highest priority or greatest interest. I suggest you limit your categories to five. While the category possibilities are numerous and in large measure depend on your unique working environment and style, some are commonplace and apply to nearly any situation.

Sample Time Log Categories

Meetings	Plant visits
Correspondence	Dictation
Telephone	Civic activities
Planning	Interruptions
Traveling/commuting	Sales calls
Socializing	Service calls
Reading	Drop-ins
Paper work	Day-dreaming

Once you have selected the five time log categories you want to use in your time analysis, write them on a piece of paper in the format following. Think about each category in turn and ask yourself this question, "What percentage of time do I spend in this category of activity in an average workday?" When you have an estimated percentage you can live with, write it in the space headed *Forecast* on your form. Complete the exercise for each of your selected categories.

	Category	*Forecast*	*Optimal*
1.	_____	_____	_____
2.	_____	_____	_____
3.	_____	_____	_____
4.	_____	_____	_____
5.	_____	_____	_____

Once you have filled in the estimated time you spend in each of your categories, decide what might be an optimal amount of time you could spend in each category. For example, you may now estimate that you spend 20 percent of your time doing paperwork and only 5 percent of your time touring your plant operations. However, given your priorities, you recognize that the percentages above should be reversed—you would like to spend more time in the plant and less time doing paperwork. Write in the estimated percentage of time you would like to spend in each category in the *Optimal* column.

After you have selected categories and have estimated your forecast and optimal time percentages, you are ready to begin logging your time. Logging or recording your time is a simple process of entering activity data, by category, on a time log form. In order to gather enough information to provide a worthwhile analysis, you will want to capture four key bits of information on each task or activity:

1. The time of entry
2. A description of the activity(ies) recorded for each entry
3. The number of minutes spent on each activity
4. The priority (A, B, C, or D) of each activity recorded

The following example represents entries made to a working time log covering the first 2½ hours of a business day. You will see how and where each of the preceding data items are entered on the log. Notice the entries are made every fifteen to thirty minutes during the period. As you inventory your own time, you will be stopping the work flow every thirty minutes or less to record information on the activities you have been involved in since the last entry.

At the conclusion of at least five working days of faithfully keeping your time log, you should do your analysis. Start by adding up the number of minutes in each category for each day. Divide the total minutes for each day into the total minutes for

TIME LOG

Start Time 8:00 **Categories** **Date** 10 - 14 - 90 KEY INFORMATION

Entry Time	PLANNING	INTER-RUPTIONS	MEETINGS	PROJECTS	PHONE	OTHER
8:15	DTL 10/A					
8:40		FRED NEED HELP 10/A		REVIEW OUTLINE 15/A		
9:00				DICTATE BLUEPRINT 20/A		
9:25		SANDY DROP BY 10/D			CHECK ON ABSENTEES 5/B	READ & SORT MAIL 10/C
10:00				OUTLINE REPORT 35/A		
11:00			STAFF MTG. 60/C			
11:25		PHONE REQUEST 5/C			CALLED WAREHSE. 10/B	TALKED TO BOSS 10/B
12:00				FINISH REPORT 20/A	TALKED WITH SHOP 10/C	
1:00						LUNCH 60/D

each category, giving a percentage for each category. Also, add the total number of minutes spent in each category that you designated as A, B, C, or D priority and write the respective numbers in the space provided at the bottom of your log sheet. Finally, combine and average percentages of each log sheet into a complete profile. Here is an example:

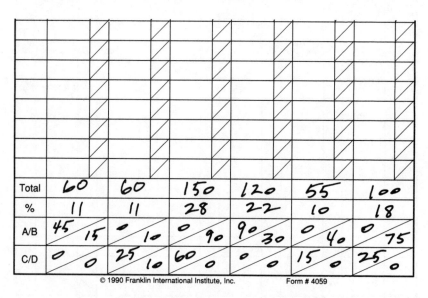

© 1990 Franklin International Institute, Inc.   Form # 4059

ANALYZING THE RESULTS

Now that your time log information has been computed and displayed in a way that is easy to read and understand, consider what you have learned about your usage of time that can help you be in better control of events. You may want to consider these questions:

- Do log results show that you are working toward important company objectives?
- What appears to be your most significant time management problem?
- What tasks on your log could, and perhaps should, have been delegated to your subordinates?
- Were you more productive in the morning hours or the afternoon hours?
- Should you start work earlier? Stay later?
- Could certain tasks have been batched and scheduled to a more appropriate time slot?
- What was the longest period of time without an interruption?

WHAT TWO OR THREE THINGS COULD YOU DO NOW TO GAIN BETTER CONTROL OF EVENTS?

Using the information revealed by the time log analysis and the questions outlined above, formulate a number of time management goals to help you reach an optimum balance between the categories and to increase focus on your "must-do" tasks. The following are examples of problem situations and possible solutions.

Situation	Solution
1. Too many C/D task minutes vs. A/B task minutes	Prioritize daily tasks. Reduce number of low priority tasks. Avoid procrastination of A/B tasks.
2. Too much time spent on low priority interruptions.	Plan short one-on-one meetings with frequent interrupters. Shorten time spent with drop-in visitors.
3. Too much time spent in ineffective meetings.	Ask for agendas of meetings in advance. Get subordinates to attend if appropriate. Ask for minutes of meetings you will not attend.
4. Many hours unaccounted for.	Could be preoccupation or not making log entries frequently enough. Run log for one day making entries every fifteen minutes.

COMMENTS ON TIME LOG USAGE

The time log is a great tool for determining how you spend your time. However, it is only as good as the data you record and the analysis done on the recorded data. Keep these important points in mind:

1. Don't try to make yourself look effective by cheating on times, activities, or priorities. The closer your time inventory represents reality, the more useful the log results will be to you.
2. Don't wait for a "typical" week to run your log. There is no such animal.
3. Don't impose the time log on your subordinates. If you do so, they will likely fill out their logs on Friday just before they are to be submitted. You will find that you have the most effective team in the world (at least on paper).
4. Do recommend the time log to selected subordinates as a self-analysis tool. Only review the results if you are invited to do so.
5. Do run your time log again in three to six months. If you have implemented your plan well, you should see significant changes in your personal productivity. After that, keep a log handy and track yourself occasionally. You'll find it a worthwhile way to provide urgency to time effectiveness.
6. Don't get discouraged. Do your log for five full working days before doing your analysis. You may want to consider starting on Thursday and finishing up on Wednesday. In spite of your feelings to the

contrary, the log will only take ten to fifteen minutes a day to fill out—time well invested.

We will close this chapter with a very important quote from Peter Drucker on the subject of time analysis:

Time is the scarcest resource, and unless it is managed, nothing else can be managed. The analysis of one's time, moreover, is the one easily accessible and yet systematic way to analyze one's work and to think through what really matters in it. "Know thyself," the old prescription for wisdom, is almost impossibly difficult for mortal man. But everyone can follow the injunction "Know thy time" if he wants to, and be well on the road toward contribution and effectiveness.

8

Controlling Procrastination

Procrastination (of vital tasks) is a close relative of incompetence and a handmaiden of inefficiency.

Alec MacKenzie

Of all self-inflicted, time management ills, procrastination looms as the most obvious, and most often readily admitted. It's a major league time-robber that affects all of us to one degree or another. To some, procrastination is a casual visitor, to others he is a near-constant companion. To all, overcoming procrastination or significantly reducing its impact means giant steps in gaining control.

In my experience and observation (and I should point out that I have had momentous experience with procrastination!) procrastination comes to us in two general ways:

Conscious—where we are "awake" and aware of what we are doing.

Unconscious—where we are almost totally unaware of our actions.

Conscious procrastination is easiest to identify, categorize, and offer specific responses to. Unconscious procrastination is a little more difficult—because we must "catch" ourselves doing it. Whether conscious or unconscious, however, we pay a heavy price for this time-robber. "Putting it off" has probably produced more heartache and failure than all other time management problems combined.

Arnold Bennett once said:

You cannot waste tomorrow; it is kept for you. You cannot waste the next hour; it is kept for you. You have to live in this twenty-four hours of daily time. Out of it you have to spin wealth, pleasure, money, content, respect, and the evolution of your immortal soul. Its right use, its most effective use, is a matter of highest urgency . . . all depends on that.

What do we lose when we procrastinate? We lose life! We lose opportunity. We lose today. To the procrastinator, "tomorrow" is a convenient cubbyhole in which to put important tasks. As a result, he wastes the present. We can learn from the past and plan for the future, but the playing field of life is today. To get into a cycle of wasting "todays" is to ensure unfulfilled tomorrows.

Procrastinators also suffer in other, cruel ways. By waiting for the last minute they are often the ones plagued by anxiety and stress. It's true that we can "put off" our life dreams and personal achievement, but on the job there are deadlines to be met. Pressures mount. The momentary "peace" that comes with pushing events into the future turns to discomfort when we realize the impact of our inaction.

Procrastinators suffer through poor careers because they miss opportunities. Clients don't get called back in a timely manner—or perhaps not at all. Excuses for late reports and projects begin to brand the procrastinator for what he is. Opportunity knocks just as often for the procrastinator as for anyone else. The procrastinator doesn't answer the door. The procrastinator may even eventually suffer from poor health. Medical and dental examinations or other necessary visits to the doctor are not pleasant experiences—so appointments never get made. Besides, we can always do it tomorrow.

WHY DO WE PROCRASTINATE?

Why do we often allow the things that matter most to be at the mercy of things that matter least?

THE UNPLEASANT TASK

William James, the father of American psychology, refers to something he calls the ''Pleasure Principle.'' Simply stated, it means that human behavior can often be determined or accounted for because we have a tendency to move toward those things that are pleasurable. It also goes without saying that we avoid things that are not pleasurable or not pleasant.

Though unpleasant to us, some distasteful but vital tasks must be done. I don't know of anyone who enjoys taking out the garbage—but we do it anyway. Think of the ugly situation that would result if *someone* didn't take out the garbage from time to time. Likewise, some folks *hate* to balance their checkbooks, fill out monthly reports, do their taxes, meet new people, speak before a group, etc. Is there a way to make unpleasant tasks into pleasant ones? Yes. Delegation. However, delegation is not always an option open to us, in which case the answer is no. There are some techniques to help us overcome the unpleasantness long enough for us to accomplish the task and put it behind us. Next time you feel the need to procrastinate a vital task, consider these suggestions.

Set a Deadline

A deadline is an urgency. Faced with a deadline we tend to move quicker and with more energy.

Challenge yourself by saying, "I will finish this in the next hour and I will not sit down (or whatever) until it is completed!" A closely related technique is called "scheduled procrastination." Here, you schedule on your appointment page a specific time to work on the project or task—then allow yourself to procrastinate until that time (but no further!).

Do the Most Unpleasant Part First

My youngest son, Steve, finds most green vegetables unpleasant and unnecessary. His mother, however, considers these menu items vital and continues to put them on Steve's dinner plate for him to eat and thereby be nourished. Steve's dinner tactic is to eat everything on his plate that he likes (remember the pleasure principle?) then fuss and stew over the necessity to consume the "ugly greenies." An obviously better approach to the "greenies" would be to eat them first, getting them out of the way so he can enjoy the remainder of his meal. Steve hasn't learned this approach. Maybe someday he'll read this book!

For us, starting with the most unpleasant part of a task makes good sense, too. We are at a higher level of energy at the beginning of a task and therefore better able to attack the unpleasantries with vigor. Put the "ugly whatevers" behind you quickly.

Make a Game of It

Turning the unpleasant task into a game is a great way to counter unpleasantness. There are various games to consider. You can play alone, or you can involve someone else—it's usually more fun to play games with someone else. The following fun (and effective) way to get kids to clean up their toys or their rooms works well with any task.

Beat the Clock

"Julie, I'm going to time you to see how fast you can get all these toys put into the toy box. Bet you can do it in less than five minutes! Don't start before I say go! Are you ready? Go!" (Stand back!)

"Boy, I still haven't gotten my monthly sales report faxed in. I'm going to get that sucker done in the next half hour and get it off my back!"

Build In a Reward

Here's a simple idea. Plan a reward for yourself (or someone else you're trying to motivate) for when you (or they) finish the dreaded task. Your reward could be a walk to the lunchroom for ice cream, an enjoyable telephone call, a relaxing moment, a new tennis racket or pair of shoes, etc. (Make sure your reward is commensurate with the size of the task you've overcome.) We should be rewarded for controlling procrastination.

OVERWHELMING TASKS

Tasks are overwhelming because of size, duration, or complexity. It's so much more enjoyable to work on a task that is quick, easy, and fun. So, break down overwhelming tasks into bite-sized pieces (how do you eat an elephant?). It's a simple idea that anyone can do and it works like magic. "Nothing is particularly hard if you divide it into small jobs," said Henry Ford. Ford's assembly line concept was built on this idea.

Writing a complex, project status report can take hours. Such a task can seem overwhelming for various reasons, but if we break it down into a series of smaller steps it becomes much less intimidating:

> Title report
> Do rough outline
> Do rough draft
> Do final draft
> Do proof

This project report could be broken down into smaller and smaller activities as needed. Slice it up! Edwin Bliss, author of the delightfully effective book *Getting Things Done*, calls this idea the "salami technique."

A Salami in its original state, before it has been cut, is unwieldy and looks unappetizing. Cut into thin slices it takes on quite a different aspect. Now you have something manageable, something you can 'get your teeth into'.

Getting Started

The procrastination gorilla is alive and well. If you have a task that is overwhelming and, therefore, unpleasant you will tend to procrastinate it. Now the gorilla begins to grow. The more you rationalize and delay the task the bigger the gorilla gets, until the anxiety you feel about the task is totally out of proportion to the problem. The way to fix the problem is to *begin* the task. The moment you begin the project, the gorilla reduces to its original, often play-toy size. How often have you procrastinated a project because you knew you were going to hate it, only to find out that, once begun, it wasn't really that bad after all?

OTHER REASONS WE PROCRASTINATE

1. *Overcommitting has a paralyzing effect.* When we fail to anticipate the effect of always agreeing to take on new responsibilities, we end up doing nothing. Make sure your time availability will accommodate a new project before you take it on. Be realistic in estimating time needed to complete tasks.

2. *Lack of information.* We can't start or continue because we still need data. Decisions can't be reached. We'll just have to wait. Whose problem is it? If it's yours, get the information you need and get on with it. If someone else is the blockage, impose urgency on the procrastinator. If waiting is the only viable alternative, switch to the next highest priority task.

3. *Unclear goals.* Someone once said that "if you don't know where you're going you may already be there!" Start being specific with yourself about long- and short-range personal objectives. As my son would say, "Get a life!"

4. *Fear of failure.* Oddly, perfectionists are really good at procrastinating. Most problems do not need perfect answers—they need action with appropriate forethought. We learn from making mistakes. Get on with it.

5. *Now is not the time.* How many times have I heard employees say such things as "Mondays (today is Monday) are not real good times to make sales calls" or "People usually aren't interested in our products during the holidays." (Now it's December.) This is classic reactive behavior. There are no bad times for you to achieve and to proceed with enthusiasm toward

your worthy objectives. Put yourself in control.

6. *General disorganization.* A cluttered and disorganized workspace can have a detrimental effect on overall productivity. Take some time to clean up that mess and put things in order. If you don't know where to begin, see chapter 10.

Keep your antenna up and be constantly aware of your own tendency to procrastinate. Remember the natural law of procrastination:

We tend to avoid events which are unpleasant, complex, lengthy or uninteresting, regardless of the priority.

9

Controlling Interruptions

Don't be defeated by a self-fulfilling prophecy that your interruptions can't be controlled. To control interruptions, analyze the cause, then apply some common sense and a positive attitude.

Jack D. Ferner

Whenever a group of people assemble to discuss problems in time management and personal productivity, "interruptions" surfaces as the most common and most annoying time-robber. We are so aware of those unwanted telephone calls and of people dropping by for a chat when we are heavily involved in a high-priority task. While we outwardly endure interruptions, we most often inwardly resent the intrusion. Interruptions are unscheduled events.

In seminars, I often ask small meeting groups to suggest ways of handling interruptions. The results are quite often a long, mostly predictable list of tactics, designed to ward off, ignore, or cut short any infringement on our time. The object of the exercise is interpreted to mean "How do we get rid of people?" I suppose so we can keep our noses to the productivity grindstone.

While it is true that some interruptions are unnecessary and unwarranted, some are very necessary and key not only to our own productivity but also to the productivity of our organizations as well. In addition, most of us have as part of our job responsibilities the implied assignment of responding to the needs of the organization around us.

WE ARE PAID TO BE INTERRUPTED

For most of us, if we didn't have an interruption for two straight days we wouldn't have a job. Fact is, interruptions are an important part of business life. The real question about interruption control is "How quickly can we spot a high-priority interruption?" and "How quickly can I recognize a dysfunctional interruption?"

Interruptions come in three flavors:

1. *Unnecessary.* The unnecessary interruption is when someone drops by or calls you on

the telephone having clearly mistaken you for someone who cares, who has information, or who has responsibility. None of these things being true, it's an unnecessary intrusion. This is a priority D interruption—a waste of time. This interruption is to be avoided or terminated quickly.

2. *Necessary.* Here is an interruption you do care about, have information about, or responsibility for. It is a priority A, B, or C. It has value. Move to handle this interruption—unless it is untimely.

3. *Untimely.* The untimely interruption is a necessary one, but it comes at an inappropriate time. Reschedule this interruption to a more suitable time.

Consider for a moment that you have an invisible balance scale on the front of your desk. This scale has two pans and in one rests the task priority you are currently working on.

When the telephone rings or someone drops into your workspace for a visit, you want to determine as quickly as possible what type of interruption it is. In a sense, you want to put the interruption on the pan opposite your current task and see how it balances out. If the interruption "weighs" more than your current task, you may want to shift your attention to the higher priority.

Obviously, if the interruption is of no value or has a lower value than your current task, you will want to dismiss it or reschedule it to a more appropriate time.

The difficult part for most people is determining the priority level of the interruption, and doing so early enough in the conversation so that adjustments can be made quickly and graciously.

THE POINT QUESTION

One of the most effective tools for determining the type or priority of an interruption is the use of the "Point Question." The point question is a simple, nonthreatening query designed to get to the point of the interruption quickly and appropriately so you, the interruptee, can take necessary action. The question can take many forms, but most commonly it asks:

> "What can I do for you?"
> "What brings you around this way?"
> "How may I help you?"
> "What is it you need?"

These phrases can be easily combined with a cheerful, outgoing greeting. "Hey, Carol, nice to see you. How can I help you today?"

The point question can work wonders. Here's why: When a person interrupts you, they seldom begin by telling you what type of interruption (necessary, unnecessary, untimely) they are. So you ask the point question to find out. In essence you are transferring "ownership" of the conversation over to the interrupting person. The subtle, underlying message is for them to quickly justify their interruption. They respond with their need or question, you instantly evaluate the priority and the time necessary to respond to the question or need, then act accordingly.

Here's an example. You are sitting at your desk involved in an urgent and important task that must be completed by 3 p.m. today. It is now 1:30 p.m. You will need most of your available time to meet the deadline. In the midst of your work, the telephone rings. You answer it and on the other end is a co-worker from another department who starts the conversation like this:

"Hey, Janet, this is Toby. How ya doin'?"

"I'm fine, Toby. Thanks. *What can I do for you?*"

"Well, at lunch last week you said you wanted to get together to discuss the safety committee meeting with me. I've got a couple of hours available now and thought it might be a good time for you."

"Toby, I'm anxious to hear about the meeting, but at the moment I'm up against an important deadline. Can we make it tomorrow shortly after lunch?"

"That sounds good to me. How about if I drop by about one thirty?"

"One-thirty will be fine. See you then."

Notice that the above conversation started with a comment that was going nowhere. Janet's "point question" got Toby to the point and Janet was then able to control her action based on the type of interruption (untimely). Since the interruption was a lower priority than Janet's current task, it was swiftly and appropriately handled. If the interruption were a higher, more urgent task than Janet's current task, she would probably have quickly adapted and responded to the interruption.

Sometimes an interruption can be easily handled even if it is a lower priority than the current task. It may be easier to handle it immediately and quickly to avoid rescheduling. Let's put Janet back in her office and have her handle just such an interruption. This time a co-worker drops by and interrupts for no apparent reason:

> "Hi, Janet. What's going on?"
> "Hi, Lynn. I'm trying to finish this report for the finance committee. *What can I do for you?*"
> "Oh, not much. I wondered if you have a copy of the new vacation policy?"
> "Sure. Hang on." (Janet gets the memo.) "Here you go. *Was there anything else?*"
> "No, thanks for the memo. I'll make a copy and get back to you. See ya!"

Again the interruption was handled with dispatch—thanks to the point question. Otherwise, it might have turned into a lengthy, unproductive social call. Notice in the above example that Janet used a second "point question" when she handed the memo copy to Lynn.

AVOIDING UNTIMELY INTERRUPTIONS

We always want to avoid unnecessary, meaningless interruptions. However, sometimes it is not that the interruption is unnecessary, but that it is untimely. Constant use of the point question could wear a little thin with co-workers and subordinates if you tried to determine the priority of each in a series of interruptions. Also, interruptions on the job are usually the result of legitimate problems or questions that affect the productivity of the organization in some way. Hiding from or avoiding these interruptions simply delays, and sometimes magnifies, the problem.

Andrew Grove, president of Intel Corporation and author of the book *High Output Management* says this about interruptions on the job:

> Understand that interrupters have legitimate problems that need to be handled. That's why they're bringing them to you. But you can channel the time needed to deal with them into an organized scheduled form by providing an alternative to interruption—a scheduled (one-on-one) meeting.

The solution suggested by Grove is a technique he calls "batching." Batching is setting a pattern of short one-on-one meetings where subordinates, and others, may ask questions or discuss problems openly, free from distractions. If subordinates or co-workers know they will have a fifteen-minute meeting with you twice weekly, they are much less apt to interrupt in the meantime unless the question or problem is of high priority and has a certain level of urgency attached to it. In other words, a necessary interruption.

OPPORTUNITY KNOCKS
(AND RINGS AND VISITS)

Interruptions should be viewed from the standpoint of our total responsibility. Not only are you paid to be interrupted, but many times the result of a necessary interruption will mean the difference between success and failure in a task or project. You are in better control of events when you know how to evaluate and appropriately respond to interruptions. Avoiding interruptions is the last resort.

YOU AS THE INTERRUPTER

One last thought about interruptions. We are often the person doing the interrupting. When you know you are interrupting another person, be sure to keep the following points in mind:

1. *Always ask if "now" is a convenient time.* You might say, "Nancy, this is Jim. I need to talk with you for about five minutes about the Williamson project. Is this a good time for you?"
2. *Plan your interruption carefully.* Know how long it will take to get or give the information. You can even make up a mini-agenda if there's more than one or two items.
3. *Never take more time than is necessary. Never* give anyone a reason to use a point question on you!

10

War on Clutter

With the elimination of clutter, things become less complicated, important connections between events are more easily seen, and the significance of experiences more readily comes home to us. What is of real importance stands out more clearly.

Milton Mayeroff

When Milton Mayeroff penned the words quoted above, he made reference to mental clutter: our tendency to clutter up our minds with unnecessary or meaningless information which keeps us from focusing on the most important matters. Mayeroff uses the analogy of static on the radio to illustrate the point in that clutter, like static, distorts the real picture or signal from the thought processes that bring about the best results. As I read Mayeroff's analogy I was struck by how closely this concept relates to actual clutter in the workspace and in our living space as well.

People have varying ideas about how clear a desk or workspace ought to be. It is a matter of personal preference and habit to be sure. However, it is nevertheless a fact that a well-organized workspace will facilitate productivity. Research has shown that our feelings of self-worth are affected directly by the order of our surroundings. We should each periodically evaluate our work environment with an eye toward determining our "clutter factor." Is it obvious to you when looking at your workspace which papers or tasks are of the highest priority? Is your workspace organized so that you know in what place the highest priority task material is located?

It is important to note that you're the most important element in your workspace. Consequently, those things of greatest importance should be closest to you and those things of lesser value should be further away.

Your highest priority space is the space closest to you.

Consider the workspace schematic that follows. Notice that specific areas of this hypothetical office have been given a priority designation. The space closest to the place the person would sit is given an A priority, while those areas at arm's length or in side drawers have been designated B spaces. C spaces can only be approached by standing up or moving to them. D space is your wastebasket. I do not believe that every workspace or desk needs to be completely clear of all but the current task. Such a standard is usually not practical. However, placement of material and equipment on your desk should reflect its priority. Most workspace clutter consists of paperwork—memos, reports, mail, etc. One of the best ways to get and keep a workspace in productive order is something I call the "Prioritized Stacking Technique." This idea is adapted from Alan Lakein.

PRIORITIZED STACKING

Remove all unorganized papers from desk drawers, *In* baskets, *Hold* baskets, etc., and stack them all on the front of your desk in your A space. Likewise, accumulate all papers from your desk top and place them on your stack. Now, stand up! (Standing serves two purposes: One, you will move faster and be less tolerant with low priority material while standing; and two, you'll probably have to stand to reach the top of your stack!) As you go through your paper, ask, "Is this an A, B, C, or D item?"

A = Must be done—*Critical*
B = Should be done—*Important*
C = Could be done—*Low Value*
D = Waste—*No Value*

If you recognize the paper as an A, put it in an A stack. Likewise, if it is a B, put it in the B stack. C's go in the C stack. Obviously, if the paper is a D, it goes in the wastebasket. (You'll have a lot of these, so you may want to borrow an additional large basket!)

If you are undecided as to whether a paper represents a C or a D, it's a D! Be ruthless. Most people have a tendency to save more than is necessary or useful.

Continue the process of prioritizing until your first stack has been replaced by A, B, and C stacks. Now act on your stacks in accordance with your workspace priority. The bulk of your papers will be in the C stack. (Remember the "vital few" versus the "trivial many.") Get these into the bottom drawer of your file cabinet or into your credenza. The B's should go into a file folder marked *Important* or B. This folder can remain on your desk or be in a desk file drawer where it can be easily reached. The A's, your most critical tasks papers, will then go into a file folder marked *Critical* or A and sit on your desk in a place offering easy access and availability.

As paperwork continues to arrive in your workspace, set a time daily to review it and prioritize it according to the above plan. There is an old and untrue adage in time management that says that "papers should only be handled once." Like a perfectly clean desk, it is a nice idea, but also impractical and unproductive. Let me suggest a better adage.

*When you handle a piece of paper,
do something productive with it.*

You can throw it away (it's a D!), you may act on it immediately, or you can simply recognize its priority and put it into the appropriate stack. Don't pick up a paper, fondle it, sort it, and return it to the *In* basket! That's paper shuffling!

IN BASKETRY

Standard equipment for most offices is the *In* basket. This basket can be one, two, or three baskets, ostensibly for *In*, *Out*, and perhaps *Hold*. If your *In* basket doesn't include a *Hold* basket then the *In* basket becomes the *Hold* basket as well.

The idea behind desk baskets is to receive incoming mail and memos and to send out the same material via messenger. It's not a bad idea, because we all need some organized method for administering the flow of paper correspondence through our workspace. However, the *In* basket can be a time management problem unless it is placed and used properly. Here are some suggestions: Do not have your *In* basket on your desk. Put the basket on your credenza, file cabinet, table, etc., if possible. If you have a secretary, your *In* basket belongs on the secretary's desk, not yours. You may consider using a drawer (upper right or left) instead of the typical *In* basket. If you must have your *In* basket on your desk, exercise self-discipline and look in the *In* basket only when you are ready to act on material placed in it. Put yourself in control of your *In* basket.

DESK CALENDARS

Beware of desk calendars! I warn you against the many varieties of plastic-based, two-metal-ringed, one-page-per-day calendars that have for some reason become a standard part of desk jewelry. Most people don't use them but keep them around out of habit. The one useful reason for having them is because they typically show the current date in bold numbers. However, this advantage is negated by the fact that they are seldom turned to the proper day!

If you currently have such a calendar on your desk, I suggest that you consider its value to you and act accordingly. If it is a valuable part of your workday, keep it. If it is a mostly forgotten piece of desk jewelry I urge you to get rid of it. A good date-book organizer such as discussed in chapter 5 would be an excellent alternative.

JUST IN CASE

We have a tendency to save and store things "just in case" we may need them sometime in the future. As a result, we seldom throw anything away. Let me suggest some simple ways for evaluating the paperwork sorted and a systematic way of reducing the amount you file and keep filed.

1. *Don't get into the habit of filing every memo that crosses your desk.* Some folks have elaborate filing systems that they are very proud of. I have had people boast that they have such a great system for filing memos that others in the office come to them when they need a copy! Unless you are charged with the duty of maintaining a memo file, don't be a librarian!

2. *Have specific titles for your file folders.* Keep the categories simple and few. Avoid having a file for "everything." Watch out for the "miscellaneous" file—if you have one, review it once a week and clear out all the D's.

3. *Files should be cleared out periodically.* Be ruthless! If you don't feel you have any short-term use for the memo or information and you are not the originator of it, *throw it away!* In spite of your inclination to say, "The minute I throw it away, someone will ask for it," the truth is, that seldom if ever happens. Also, there is certainly nothing wrong with not having a copy just because someone asks for it. Unless you are paid to do it, don't waste your precious time filing and retrieving for others.

WAR ON CLUTTER

Having a workspace that is clear of clutter and filing systems that promote simplicity and order enhances your personal productivity. You will feel better about yourself and your work will show it. Don't allow clutter to choke out the truly vital tasks and obscure the things that matter most. Make *war on clutter!* It is a continuing process that requires daily attention. If you notice things starting to pile up, invest a few minutes to bring order to your environment. Put yourself in a condition of control.

11

Working Through Others

The purpose of delegation is to transmit power from a superior to a subordinate so the latter can accomplish a necessary task.

Ross A. Webber

There is probably not a single subject that receives more emphasis in management training programs than that of how to manage, motivate, train, control, direct, or otherwise influence people. There's a good reason for this. The output of any organization is, in the final analysis, a function of how much productivity is derived from each individual in the organization. It is the vital job function of any manager to gain and sustain high

levels of effectiveness from his or her subordinates.
In fact, the whole thrust of achieving organizational objectives is tied to the fundamental people
resource.

For most managers, working with others on
day-to-day projects and tasks is the way we get
things done. In a time management context, when
we assign tasks and responsibilities to subordinates
they become agents for us in controlling events.

In this chapter we will discuss working with
others in a work-sharing or delegation framework.
Generally at first and then, near the end of the
chapter, I will give some handy suggestions for
successfully working with administrative support
people.

WHERE DO MANAGERS COME FROM?

Managers typically become managers because
they did what they did as individual contributors
very well. The best engineers commonly get promoted to engineering managers. The best sales-
people eventually wind up being a sales manager.
For most of us, our career paths worked that way
and we would have been disappointed had we
been passed over too many times for a ''management'' slot. Consequently, when we get the pro-
motion and move into the new office our main
skills are those of an individual contributor and not
a manager. As a result, many new managers fail to

manage—they continue to be detail doers instead of directing activity.

Since the skills of management are quite different from those of an individual contributor, being a new manager can be a frustrating circumstance.

DIFFICULTIES OF DELEGATION

I suppose some caveman stonecutter in eons past reached the point in his budding business where he couldn't do all the work himself. He would like to have done it all himself, because, after all, it was his business and he was the only one who knew how to cut stones. Or at least how to do it right. So he hired someone to help him. Now we have our first manager. This first manager probably didn't give the new worker much of importance to do. No autonomy. No authority. Probably he eventually grew tired of seeing someone else mess with his stuff and finally killed the worker and ate him.

I think it was much later in the evolution of business management skills that a manager had his first successful experience working with others. Learning how to manage is learning how to give. How to communicate. How to teach. How to delegate.

In today's business world, poor delegation is one of the greatest causes of management failure. Just as in the case of our ancient stonecutter, the problems could easily have been avoided by applying a few basic principles.

Controlling Events through Others

Delegation is a process of having others act for us in the accomplishment of tasks. If our delegation is to be effective from a time and results standpoint, there are certain natural laws of communication to be followed.

The bulk of this chapter will refer to delegation in management, but the concepts will work in any organizational setting—even in a family. Also, while we are not all managers, it is a fact that nearly all of us are delegatees. A delegatee, with a clear understanding of the discipline of delegation, can make a manager a better delegator. Moreover, we learn to delegate by the way we are delegated to.

Delegation is more than parceling our assignments out to subordinates. Effective delegation involves determining what work to be done is actually *ours* and then making sure that we don't find ourselves consumed by work that rightfully belongs to another. Knowing how to appropriately assign tasks, how to follow-up on work delegated, knowing when not to delegate and avoiding the common "backward delegation" trap are all vital to shared event control.

Let us first review the three major excuses for failing to delegate properly or failing to delegate at all.

1. *I like to do the work myself—then I know it's been done right.* As has been stated, you may be in your present position because you did what you did as an individual contributor very well. Consequently, you may rightfully feel that you can do a job faster and better than anyone on your staff. Whether your motivation is doing what you like to do, a feeling of indispensability, or even a fear that you have incompetent subordinates, you are likely doing tasks that belong to others. People in this situation are usually frustrated and overworked, and they should be! The solution is to recognize that as a manager, one of your vital functions is to teach and develop your staff. As Paul Meyers says, "The best way to increase your authority is to delegate it."

2. *I don't know how to delegate effectively—it never seems to work out.* Skills in delegation can be easily learned. If you sincerely lack confidence in your ability to assign tasks appropriately, carefully study the keys to effective delegation which follow. If expectations are communicated specifically, and necessary help and follow-up are provided, you'll be a better delegator than 90 percent of all managers—first time out!

3. *I feel I need to help my subordinates to meet their deadlines by lifting some of the workload.*

This is a classic example of "backward delegation." It is fine to help—by teaching. However, we do a disservice to our subordinates when we assume responsibility for tasks that are rightfully theirs. Special cases excepted, let the monkey remain on the back of the appropriate individual. Backward delegation taken to its extreme is the key to managerial burnout.

Keys to Effective Delegation

1. Delegate only if you have complete confidence in your subordinate's ability to successfully complete the task. If you lack confidence in the delegatee, you may want to assign only part of the task to be done. Another approach would be to teach your subordinate how to do the job or, better yet, assign the task jointly with another, more experienced worker.

2. Clearly define responsibility delegated. Where the instructions are verbal, ask the delegatee to "play back" the instructions —you may not have been clear. Where you can, make complex task responsibilities in writing.

4. Jointly establish deadlines and priorities. This can't always happen due to the press

of tasks and time. However, when you can, stop and ask when the subordinate could complete the tasks, given the current workload. Let them know where this new task fits into the schedule and gain commitment on a follow-up or completion time.

5. Provide feedback; be specific. As Ken Blanchard says, "Catch people doing something right!" When you receive the results of a delegated task, be quick in acknowledging a well-done job. If there are problems, be kind, but be specific in restating your original expectations. Point out the specific things about the results that were good and those that could have been improved. People love feedback.

Delegating to the "Round File"

Peter Drucker, writing in his exceptional book, *The Effective Executive*, gives us a wonderfully practical insight into productivity:

I have yet to see an executive, regardless of rank or station, who could not consign something like a quarter of the demands on his time to the wastepaper basket without anybody's noticing their disappearance.

If management can be defined as getting things done through other people, then delegation is an integral part of the management process. Developing skills as a delegator is essential to every manager.

Effective managers delegate out of necessity—the workload cannot be handled by one person. The more effective the delegation, the more events brought under control, the more productive your unit will be. Building excellence into an organization is predicated on people working together in a positive atmosphere.

WORKING SUCCESSFULLY WITH ADMINISTRATIVE PEOPLE

At the risk of offending someone, I'm going to use the word "secretary" here. Not only am I going to use the "S" word, but I'm going to use it boldly. It's unfortunate that the word "secretary" has come to mean something less than the true value of the position. My secretary has the title of executive assistant. That's nice, because she truly functions as my assistant and I am, after all, an executive. She is also an extremely effective and professional secretary.

I attended a luncheon recently where the keynote speaker made this comment:

> I find it interesting that I can take a few hours off during the week to play golf if I want or

need to, and nothing seems to suffer in my absence. I also find that if I need to be out of town for a few days that things seem to be in order upon my return. But if my secretary is away from her desk for even a few minutes, my business suffers. And if she's gone for a few days, all hell breaks loose!

Here was an executive who knew the value of his secretary and obviously how to make optimum use of this vital management resource.

Does your secretary spend most of her time working on routine stuff—typing, transcribing, filing, etc? Could she be delegated tasks of greater importance—tasks that you are currently, and perhaps inappropriately handling? Are you limiting your own effectiveness by underutilizing your assistant's time?

Aside from the obvious routine administrative tasks, I've found that professional secretaries can effectively work on independent projects, attend important meetings, prescreen reading, organize office functions, administer and even host luncheons and conferences, delegate tasks to junior people and, best of all, be the ''boss's boss.'' All this presupposes that you have the right person for the job and that she or he has the skills to carry out these assignments. But then, that's true for any key subordinate.

Also, shared secretaries are very common. If you share a secretary with another, or several other, managers, be sensitive to overburdening.

The secretary may simply not have the time to do anything but the basic functions.

Keys to Successful Boss/Secretary Partnerships

1. *Keep your secretary informed.* To an appropriate extent, your assistant should always be generally in the know on current projects and concerns—not just "Where are you?" and "When will you be back?" She should know what your plans are and what strategic goals you are working toward. Your secretary can also keep *you* informed. The "bamboo wireless" is always transmitting in any organization. Chances are your secretary is plugged in. Chances are you aren't.

2. *Have a formal meeting with your secretary at least once a day.* This is probably the most important, routine, one-on-one meeting you'll have. This is where you'll find out what's happening, get updates on your schedule, communicate issues and concerns, delegate tasks, etc. The number of informal, drop-in meetings will be greatly reduced if you take the time for such a scheduled meeting. I suggest a meeting shortly after you've done your personal planning for the day, and again later in the afternoon to wrap things up and coordinate efforts.

3. *Be consistent in scheduling.* Some managers like to make their own appointments and schedule their own time. Others rely on their secretaries totally for this function. Either method works. I know of situations where there's a combination—the manager schedules Mondays and Fridays and the secretary schedules Tuesday through Thursday. This idea can work too, but don't get too complex with scheduling or you may find that no one ends up doing it! Calendaring must be a key part of your daily administrative meetings.

12

Meeting Time

A meeting is nothing less than the medium through which managerial work is performed. That means we should not be fighting their very existence, but rather using the time spent in them as efficiently as possible.

Andrew S. Grove

Everyone meets. Staffs meet, project managers meet, new employees meet, teachers meet, ball teams meet, church groups meet, families meet, neighbors meet, people meet. Everyone meets. There is probably not a single activity more common to the day-to-day running of the millions of diverse organizations throughout the world than the practice of holding meetings. It is a simple truth that we do not "stand alone." We need to interact with others to bring about the results we seek. Organizational excellence is predicated on people working in concert with one another.

If meetings are such a necessary part of maintaining high levels of productivity and of reaching organizational objectives, then why are they so often dreaded and identified as major time-robbers by their participants? Consider this: There are no courses in business schools titled Meetings 101. What most people know about planning for, conducting or participating in meetings, they learned "on-the-job." As a result, the products of their meetings are not apt to be any better than their range of experience in meetings.

Effective meetings have a marked effect on productivity and the self-esteem of meeting leaders and participants as well. R. Dean Herrington, author of the famous *Effective Meetings Seminar* has said:

> People feel good about the time they spend in meetings in direct proportion to the quality of the products produced at those meetings.

How are "quality products" produced in a meeting? Certainly not by accident. Those meetings that achieve the most effective results are those meetings that have been appropriately planned for, scheduled, and conducted. Let's review some of the elements of planning, conducting, and participating in time effective meetings.

MEETING ROLES

In order for a meeting to be successful, the people involved in the meeting must fill certain roles effectively. There are many roles filled during the course of a meeting by each person involved. However, we will focus our attention on the key roles of Meeting Leader, Recorder, Time Keeper and, of course, Participant.

MEETING TYPES

Meetings are held for various reasons. We will discuss the five most common meeting types or purposes and how these may be integrated into a multipurpose meeting or how they may stand alone as a single meeting purpose.

MEETING METHODS

With an understanding of meeting roles and types, we will focus on the meeting methods which best serve the purpose or objective of the gathering.

MEETING PLANNING

As in time management, the key to effective meetings is in the planning process—bringing those future meeting events into the present so appropriate control can be applied. Four key meeting questions will be offered for the consideration of a meeting leader with a meeting to plan.

THE MEETING ROLES

The Meeting Leader

We typically think of the meeting leader as the one who is responsible for meeting effectiveness. While this is generally true, a more valid statement would be: "Each person in a meeting is responsible for the role he or she is assigned to fill." When each appropriately fills the role given or assumed, the meeting shows a dramatic increase in effectiveness.

The Meeting Leader is the one who plans the meeting. Meeting planning includes:

1. Preparing the agenda
2. Arranging the time and location
3. Calling or announcing the meeting

The Meeting Leader may also fill other roles in the meeting, i.e., participant, time keeper, etc. However, the major responsibility for the Meeting Leader is to direct the energy of the assembled parties to the production of planned-for results. The

Meeting Leader's vital responsibility is to conduct and control the meeting to the end.

The Recorder

The Recorder is selected by the meeting leader and has the responsibility of recording important information discussed at the meeting. The Recorder takes selective notes, not a detailed transcript of the proceedings. Key information regarding the disposition of each agenda item, delegated tasks, and decisions reached should be recorded.

Insofar as possible and practical, the notes taken by the Recorder should be displayed for all attendees of the meeting to see as they are written. A standing flip chart is an excellent medium for such notes. Since the meeting record taken by the Recorder will serve as the formal record of the experience, all involved should be able to see the notes being taken to insure accuracy. If this idea seems awkward to you, it's probably because it is new. However, in actual practice, taking a few moments following each agenda item to review the notes pertaining to it is an excellent way to gain closure and ensure understanding.

The role of the Recorder requires certain skills of listening, questioning (for clarity), and the ability to write so that others can read. The person selected for this role can be someone who will have no other responsibility in the meeting. However, in most meetings, for reasons of practicality, the Recorder is also a meeting participant.

The Time Keeper

The role of Time Keeper is, very simply, to foster time awareness within the meeting group. Periodically, and informally, the Time Keeper informs the group of how much time remains for the agenda item being considered or for the entire meeting. If time has run out or if adjustments need to be made to the agenda in the interest of time, appropriate action is taken by the Meeting Leader.

The Participant

The Participant is, of course, vital to the meeting effectiveness. One of the marks of an effective meeting is the extent to which participants actually participate in the process by asking questions and making comments. Such participating is a function of the meeting leader's ability to draw some people into the conversation and to "shut down" more verbose people, for a time. However, if a participant is well aware of the topics to be discussed in a meeting, prepares to make a contribution, and arrives on time, this crucial role will be effective even without a strong meeting leader. Furthermore, if something is not clear, or if support cannot be given to a recommendation, it is the participant's responsibility to speak up! If someone is in error on a factual matter, it should be pointed out!

Participants are invited to meetings because they have some contribution to make, an important perspective on the subjects to be discussed, or simply to be informed. Taking personal notes in the meeting is essential to remembering the important points and follow-up tasks.

MEETING TYPES

Meetings come in various flavors—in various types. It is obvious that a meeting held to gather information to be used or analyzed later will be quite a different meeting than one convened to reach a decision or to evaluate a process already in place. The time to clarify the meeting type is not after the meeting is underway, but as the meeting is being planned. In determining the meeting type, you will want to analyze the purpose of the meeting specifically, ''What do we want to gain as a result of this meeting?'' or ''What will be the end product?'' As the answers to these questions surface, they should give you an idea of the meeting type or combination of types you want used in your meeting.

Information Gathering

This meeting type is strictly for gathering or sharing of information or perspectives.

Problem Solving

A change needs to be made in a process, relationship, product, policy, etc. This meeting is for analyzing the problem.

Decision-Making

The purpose of this meeting is to reach a decision from previously determined alternatives.

Planning

Planning is bringing future events into the present so that appropriate control can be applied. So, the planning meeting is concerned with implementation plans, potential problems, etc.

Evaluation

This meeting is the guardian of a project or developing process. It is held to evaluate progress toward a specific objective—usually the result of a prior meeting.

MEETING METHODS

Several meeting methods are available to help reach meeting objectives. In selecting a method, the meeting planner should consider the meeting type and purpose, then select the best method to meet those needs.

Guided Discussion

The Guided Discussion method is probably the most widely used meeting method, and for good reason—it has a broad range of application. It is typical to staff meetings, sales meetings, personal meetings, project meetings, etc. Guided discussions are structured meetings where an agenda is used to sequence topics—each topic being covered before moving on to the next.

Round Robin

The Round Robin meeting promotes involvement from all participants by giving a time slice for reporting or information sharing to each person—usually three to five minutes. While it can be used for a short information sharing meeting, it is more typically used as a way of collecting or assessing the volume of information or the scope of alternatives before moving on to a guided discussion.

Brainstorm

The Brainstorm is a structured verbal or nonverbal, solution-seeking meeting. The idea behind this meeting type is to generate as many alternative solutions to a given problem as possible in a short period of time. Participants verbally express ideas at random while a recorder writes the ideas for evaluation later. A Brainstorm is typified by spontaneity; therefore, no critique is offered—positive or negative. Creative, outlandish suggestions are encouraged as a way of generating ideas. The Brainstorm is usually followed by a guided discussion meeting where the ideas suggested are evaluated, categorized, etc.

The nonverbal Brainstorm involves writing ideas on separate cards. At the conclusion, the written ideas are sorted and evaluated as in the verbal Brainstorm.

MEETING PLANNING QUESTIONS

Time effective meetings are a result of good planning and careful execution of the plan. Before the meeting starts, the meeting leader should be prepared to answer several questions about the meeting to be held.

What Is the Objective?

Is the meeting necessary? Is there a better way of accomplishing the purpose of the meeting than holding a meeting? You should be able to clearly state the objective of the meeting in quantifiable terms on the agenda and again at the beginning of your meeting.

What Type and Method?

Given the objective, what is the best meeting type and method for bringing about the purpose? Perhaps a combination of methods and types will work best. Plan how you intend to structure the meeting to achieve the best, most efficient results.

Who Should Attend?

This is a key question. The people you invite to the meeting should be able to accomplish the objective of the meeting. If the meeting is to reach a decision, those with authority to reach or ratify such a decision should be there. If your meeting is primarily to collect data, those "in the know" need to be there. In short, ensure that every person attending your meeting has a specific contribution to make or will receive a specific benefit as a result of being there.

What Is the Agenda?

It is a primary rule of meeting management that all participants know what to expect prior to coming to the meeting. The best way to accomplish this knowledge is to send out a specific agenda at least two days before the meeting is to be held. In addition to agenda items in their appropriate sequence, the agenda should include information on the time and location, who is calling the meeting, when the meeting will likely end, the desired outcome and materials necessary for participants to bring to the meeting. Individual assignments should be added to meeting notices as necessary.

ADDITIONAL IDEAS

1. Start on time. Do not reward latecomers by waiting for their arrival, and don't rehearse details already discussed to those who show up late. If tardiness is an ongoing problem, state the start times in your memos as "exactly 10:00 a.m." or "precisely at 10 o'clock." Emphasize promptness.

2. Stick with your agenda. Try to resolve each issue in turn or assign the responsibility to resolve an issue outside of the meeting time, if appropriate. Let the agenda be the disciplining agent in keeping the meeting in line and on time.

3. Meet standing up. Invite your participants *not* to sit down. This technique has limited application, but it can keep a short meeting from becoming a long one.

4. End on time. The exceptions to this rule occur when either the meeting can be let out early because agenda items have been satisfied, or a later "end time" is negotiated by the meeting group. Never ask the question "Is there anything else we need to discuss?" Instead, ask "Does anyone have anything to add to the next meeting's agenda?"

5. Control meeting interruptions. Have a controlled environment for your meeting that will discourage interruptions except for real emergencies.

6. Limit attendees. Most meetings do not function well if more than eight people attend. The "point of diminishing returns" enters the picture when you have more than eight. This is particularly true of decision-making meetings. Andrew Grove says, "Decision making is not a spectator sport—onlookers get in the way of what needs to be done."

13

Your Future Events—
The Challenge

If one advances confidently in the direction of his dreams, and endeavors to live the life which he has imagined, he will meet with success unexpected in common hours.

Thoreau

Throughout this book, you have been exposed to many ideas and concepts. Some of the material presented was familiar to you; some you viewed from a new perspective. Perhaps as you read through the section on value identification and goal setting you were able to catch a vision of yourself reaching out and becoming closer to the person your personal priorities suggest you are. Perhaps you saw yourself achieving a goal of significant proportions. As you learned the principles of workspace organization, did you gain a mental picture of your office as an environment of productivity— giving you flexibility and control? Maybe you were able to feel positive emotions achieved through event control. Perhaps you saw yourself reading more, spending more time with those who matter most to you, or pursuing hobbies and sports that interest you to a greater, more successful extent.

I would sincerely hope that you have had several such emotions as you have pondered the ideas expressed in the preceding chapters and that you continue to visualize the potential you have for personal achievement. As you reinforce those visions and feelings you will be led to enhance your behavior in such a way as to help you reach your goals and become what you wish to become.

There are three natural laws that deal with behavior change. Each of these laws will work to your benefit to the extent that you apply them.

1. *We Change Our Lives By Changing Our Attitudes and Perceptions.* The first step in the process has probably already begun for you as you have read through this book or experienced education in any form. Your attitude toward the subject of time management has changed. Perhaps you perceive the subject as being broader than you had imagined before. In any event, the seeds of

behavior change are sown when our attitudes and perceptions change toward a given subject or process.

2. *We Become What We Think About Ourselves.* As our perceptions and attitudes change, we begin to visualize ourselves in new roles. We see ourselves differently now, in light of the new perspective. We see ourselves as a better manager of events—we see ourselves in a higher condition of control. Once our vision of ourselves in the new role is clear, we begin to gravitate in our thoughts and actions toward the "new" person we envision, which brings us to the third natural law of behavior.

3. *Our Minds Are Naturally Goal Seeking.* With a clear picture of our objective, we *automatically* move in the direction of the change or goal—the clearer the vision of the change the more pronounced the directed action. It is a natural, eternal law of behavior that our actions are the product of our thoughts. The aphorism "As a man thinketh in his heart, so is he" is true—we literally are what we think.

The whole concept of "self-image psychology" is built upon these three natural laws. Dr. Maxwell Maltz, the most famous in his field and the author of the best-selling book on the subject, *Psycho-Cybernetics*, says:

*The moment you experience an event vividly
in the imagination it is recorded as experienced.*

In application of the three natural laws above,
Maltz suggests that we can imagine future
performances in such a way as to change them for
the better (or, alas, for the worse if we focus on the
negative and conjure up destructive attitudes and
perceptions).

Some years ago, while teaching a time management seminar, I was approached by a participant
who announced that she had recently been
promoted to vice-president of marketing for the
company she worked for. It was a large
manufacturing company and she had far-reaching
responsibilities about which she had complete
confidence. Her concern was that she had been
assigned to present her new marketing plan to the
assembled board of directors and officers of the
company in a board meeting two weeks hence. She
felt some anxiety at the prospect of giving such a
high-level presentation—particularly because this
would be the first time she would appear before
them in her new capacity. She said, "Dick, can you
give me some tips that will help me to be more
poised and effective in my presentation?" I asked
her if she knew the material she planned to present
and what media she would use. She responded
that she knew it "cold." I then suggested that she
use some *self-image psychology* to help her prepare. I
asked her to spend thirty minutes a day going over
the presentation material in her mind, imagining

herself performing each step with poise and confidence, perfecting her presentation. I asked her to visualize her audience and imagine the positive response as she made her presentation. I also suggested that she visit the site of the board meeting to gain a better picture of the environment she would make her presentation in. She agreed to do these things and to let me know how things worked out.

About two months later I received a letter of appreciation from an enthusiastic vice-president of marketing. The presentation had gone extremely well and she was very pleased with the results. In her letter she said, "I even imagined what kinds of questions the directors were apt to ask and then, in my imagination, I answered each one with poise. Do you know," she added, "three of the questions I prepared for were actually asked in the meeting!" She closed her letter by reiterating how well her presentation went, then she wrote, "And why not? I had given that presentation ten times before!"

As you prepare for reaching your objectives, whatever they may be, and invest the time in imagining the process, the newness wears off and we relegate the action to our subconscious. It becomes a habit. In fact, the natural laws given previously automatically lead us to habitualize the process for our benefit or to our detriment. James Allen writes:

> People imagine that thought can be kept secret, but it cannot; it rapidly crystallizes into habit, and habit solidifies into circumstance.

An anonymous poet has us in his debt for the following words of truth about the marvelous effect of habits.

I am your companion. I am your greatest
    helper or heaviest burden.
I will push you onward or drag you down to
    failure. I am completely at your command.
Half the things you do you might just as well
    turn over to me and I will do them—
    quickly and correctly.
I am easily managed—you must merely be
    firm with me. Show me exactly how you
    want something done and after a few
    lessons I will do it automatically.
I am the servant of all great people; and,
    alas, of all failures as well.
Those who are great, I have made great.
    Those who are failures, I have made
    failures.
I am not a machine, though I work with all
    the precision of a machine plus the
    intelligence of a person.
You may run me for profit or run me for
    ruin—it makes no difference to me.
Take me, train me, be firm with me, and I will
    place the world at your feet.
Be easy with me and I will destroy you. Who
    am I? *I am habit!*

There is no formula for developing good, productive habits. Habits will, if planted and nurtured properly, become the automatic success mechanism for making the Productivity Pyramid work for you. William James outlines, in his classic text, *The Principles of Psychology,* the four essential steps of creating habit.

1. *Demonstrate strong commitment.* Be totally committed to your resolution. Use self-talk that announces your commitment to reach your objectives. Burn the bridges that are attached to doubt and hesitancy. Consider the words of Ella Wilcox: "There is no chance, no destiny, no fate that can circumvent or hinder or control the firm resolve of a determined soul."

2. *Act on your goal at the first opportunity.* Do not procrastinate progress. Review your goals and determine what the initial or next step should be—then, take that step the first chance you get.

3. *Practice daily.* Reaching high levels of productivity is a skill that requires practice like any other developing skill. Let the realization of your goals be a daily activity. Remember that life happens day-by-day, event-by-event. Plan something today that gets you closer to your ideal. the size of the step is unimportant—the direction is all important.

4. *Never let an exception occur.* Exceptions are diversions and roadblocks. Don't allow them unless and until your new habit is firmly rooted and is in your comfort zone. Diversions should be short and planned for — don't lose sight of your objective.

A FINAL WORD

Gaining and maintaining appropriate control of events is a noble and attainable pursuit that will aid you in achieving success in whatever objectives you envision. Even though I have had to include application specifics and certain technicalities of process in this book, I have tried to paint with a brush broad enough so that underlying principles are not obscured. Also, I have tried to avoid the "author" tendency to prescribe values or behavior that I consider correct. My challenge, rather, was to provide insight to your potential for reaching personal fulfillment for yourself within the framework of your highest values and your loftiest goals. If I have been even slightly successful in meeting my challenge, your challenge is to begin.

Whatever you can do, or dream
you can — begin it!

Goethe

Bibliography

Allen, James. *As a Man Thinketh.* Salt Lake City: Bookcraft.

Bennett, Robert F. *Gaining Control.* Salt Lake City: Franklin International Institute, Inc., 1987.

Blanchard, Kenneth, and Spencer Johnson. *The One Minute Manager.* New York: William Morrow and Co., 1982.

Bliss, Edwin C. *Getting Things Done.* New York: Charles Scribner's Sons, 1976.

Branden, Nathaniel. *The Psychology of Self-Esteem.* Los Angeles: Nash Publishing Corp., 1969.

Covey, Stephen R. *How to Succeed with People.* Salt Lake City: Deseret Book Company, 1972.

Dewey, John. *Experience and Education.* London: Macmillan Publishing Inc., 1938.

Drucker, Peter F. *The Effective Executive.* New York: Harper and Row Publishers, 1969.

Ferner, Jack D. *Successful Time Management.* New York: John Wiley and Sons, 1980.

Franklin, Benjamin. *Autobiography.* London: Macmillan Publishing, Inc.

Gardner, John W. *Excellence.* New York: Harper and Row Publishers, 1962.

Glasser, William. *Reality Therapy.* New York: Harper and Row Publishers, 1975.

Goble, Frank G. *The Third Force.* New York: Simon and Schuster, 1971.

Gordon, Thomas. *Leader Effectiveness Training.* New York: Wyden Books, 1987.

Grove, Andrew S. *High Output Management.* New York: Random House, 1983.

Herrington, R. Dean. *Effective Meetings.* Houston: The Herrington Group.

James, William. *Psychology.* London, Collier-Macmillan Ltd., 1962.

Kiev, Ari. *A Strategy for Daily Living.* New York: The Free Press, 1973.

Lakein, Alan. *How to Get Control of Your Time and Your Life.* New York: The New American Liberty, Inc., 1974.

LeBoeuf, Michael. *Working Smart.* New York: McGraw-Hill Book Co., 1979.

MacKenzie, R. Alec. *The Time Trap.* New York: McGraw-Hill, 1960.

Maltz, Maxwell. *Psycho-Cybernetics.* New York: Prentice-Hall, 1960.

Maxwell, Neal A. *A More Excellent Way.* Salt Lake City: Deseret Book Company, 1973.

Meyer, Paul J. *The Dynamics of Personal Leadership.* Waco, Texas: Success Motivation Institute, 1965.

Newman, James W. *Release Your Brakes.* New York: Warner Books, 1977.

Peters, Thomas J. and Robert H. Waterman, Jr. *In Search of Excellence.* New York: Harper and Row, 1982.

Selye, Hans. *Stress without Distress.* New York: The New American Liberty, Inc., 1974.

Webber, Ross A. *A Guide to Getting Things Done.* New York: The Free Press, 1980.

Winston, Stephanie. *The Organized Executive.* New York: Warner Books, 1983.

Index